FORCE OF NATURE

LAIRD HAMILTON

FORCE of NATURE

MIND, BODY, SOUL,
AND, OF COURSE,
SURFING

RODALE®

© 2008 by Laird Hamilton

Rodale books may be purchased for business or promotional use or for special sales.
For information, please write to:
Special Markets Department, Rodale Inc., 733 Third Avenue, New York, NY 10017

Printed in the United States of America
Rodale Inc. makes every effort to use acid-free ♾, recycled paper ♻.

Interior photo credits appear on page 235

Book design by Christopher Rhoads

Library of Congress Cataloging-in-Publication Data

Hamilton, Laird.
     Force of nature : mind, body, soul (and, of course, surfing) / Laird Hamilton.
          p.   cm.
     Includes bibliographical references.
     ISBN-13 978–1–59486–942–6   hardcover
     ISBN-10 1–59486–942–1   hardcover
     1. Health.   2. Conduct of life   3. Surfing.   I. Title.
     RA776.5.H2565   2008
     613—dc22   2008034811

Distributed to the trade by Macmillan

2   4   6   8   10   9   7   5   3   1   hardcover

RODALE
LIVE YOUR WHOLE LIFE™

We inspire and enable people to improve their lives and the world around them
For more of our products visit **rodalestore.com** or call 800-848-4735

For JoAnn, Gabby, Izabela, Reece, and Brody

My Loves

TWENTY YEARS FROM NOW YOU WILL BE
MORE DISAPPOINTED BY THE THINGS YOU
DIDN'T DO THAN BY THE ONES YOU DID DO.
SO THROW OFF THE BOWLINES. SAIL AWAY
FROM THE SAFE HARBOR. CATCH THE
TRADE WINDS IN YOUR SAILS. EXPLORE.
DREAM. DISCOVER.

—MARK TWAIN

CONTENTS

It's a big world. And we humans? Not so big. If you put yourself into a position where you realize that in your solar plexus, one thing I can promise is that you'll never feel more alive. For some of us, it doesn't take leaping off a cliff. It could be a high porch. It's all relative.

Our days are meant to be fun. Once you lose that thread, I think you've just lost the essence of the whole deal. If you build up a wealth of experiences, letting yourself be amazed by everything and everyone around you, then fun and its close relative, joy, will be the inevitable by-products. The last thing you want to do is to look back at the end and think *coulda, woulda, shoulda.*

The idea is to become an old wizard; to live a long and fruitful life and have family and be healthy and enjoy the ride. And speaking of the ride, why not let it rip, at least a little bit? Everyone I know who's really stoked about getting out of bed in the morning does that to some extent.

What you can do, only you can imagine. Albert Einstein (who, as you know, was a pretty smart guy) said, "Imagination is greater than reality." For each of us, reality is as wide and as open as our imaginations will allow it to be. On the pages that follow, I've described some of the ideas, strategies, and philosophies that have worked in my life. Though we're all different, and ultimately we all need to write our own playbooks, I hope there's something in my journey that might inspire you in yours.

Life is for living.

ACKNOWLEDGMENTS

Writing a book has something in common with big-wave surfing: It takes a team to make sure everything turns out right. My deepest thanks go to Susan Casey and to my manager, Jane Kachmer. I'd also like to send some aloha to Sloan Harris of ICM and to Karen Rinaldi, Shannon Welch, Leigh Haber, Chris Rhoads, and the entire Rodale team. Many friends and colleagues generously gave their time and their expertise to this project, and their contributions are deeply appreciated: Dave Kalama, Brett Lickle, Don Wildman, Don King, T. R. Goodman, Paul Chek, Gerry Lopez, Rob Machado, Giada De Laurentiis, Nate Heydari, Neil ElAttrache, Nadia Toraman, Keri and Ed Stewart, Tom Servais, Sylvain Cazenave, Kurt Markus, Sonny Miller, Jeff Hornbaker, David Turnley, Sam Jones, Dave Homcy, Erik Aeder, Tim McKenna, Darrell Wong, Davis Factor, John Russell. And thank you to all the people who inspire me so I can hopefully inspire others.

We're all human, which means we all have the same opportunities and the same struggles. It's all about that voice inside our head that we call our mind—what it leads us to believe determines how we act and how our lives unfold. Which is why when I catch myself thinking bleak thoughts, I'll go out and do something physically strenuous, like clear brush or move rocks or paddle down the coast.

I believe that our thoughts have real, powerful effects on us. For instance, let's say you wake up one morning in a rotten mood. You don't know why, but you're just looking for a fight. Well, in my experience, the moment you walk out your front door you're going to find

PART 1
MIND

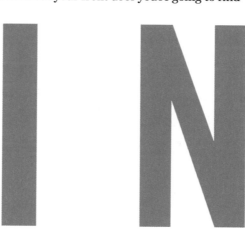

someone who wants to fight you back. He'll probably be standing right there. On the other hand, if you're just thinking about enjoying yourself, you're probably not running into a lot of complications. Everything comes down to attitude: You determine what yours is, and the external world will reflect it back.

Whether that's good news or bad news depends on you—on your outlook. If you think you're not able to do something, guess what? You're right. What if you believe that everything's for the best and see the beauty all around you, and you have faith that things will be good? You're right, too. If you cultivate something in your mind, you give it a life. It's really that simple.

RISK AND ITS REWARDS

A LITTLE ADRENALINE EVERY DAY KEEPS THE BOREDOM AWAY.

When I was 10, my stepfather took me to Waimea Falls on Oahu. I walked to the edge of a 60-foot cliff, and when he looked away, I jumped. For whatever reason, from the start it's been in my spirit to do those kinds of things. I've always wanted to jump from the highest place, experience the greatest thrill.

I may be an extreme case, but we all need to take risks. I think it goes back to our primitive state, our deepest DNA, when we were hunters and had to avoid getting eaten by large animals. Survival meant risk. The need for adventure is part of human nature. It's in every cell of our bodies. When some people hear the word *risk*, they think of life-or-death situations that they'd rather avoid. But risk doesn't always have to be life threatening. It can be as simple as putting yourself in an unfamiliar situation.

Some people don't need to go out of their way to seek risk. If you live in Afghanistan, for instance, you're not in need of any extra uncertainty. But for those of us who are fortunate enough to live in places where our lives are relatively safe, I think if we challenged ourselves—even scared ourselves—once a day, we'd be better people. It helps to have that little jolt of perspective to remind you that life's fragile.

The distinction between being courageous and being reckless is an important one. "Courageous" means you're able to calculate what you're doing. In my life I've taken calculated risks, as well as inadvertent risks. I've seen 18-foot-long tiger sharks in the water with me; I've been trapped under waterfalls. My mom was surprised that I made it to my 20th birthday. I guess it's the whole nine lives thing. There were a few close calls, but I'm still here. I've got a few of those nine lives left.

Teahupoo, Tahiti
August 17, 2000

DEALING WITH *FEAR* AND *NEGATIVITY*

MAKE SURE YOUR WORST ENEMY DOESN'T LIVE BETWEEN YOUR OWN TWO EARS.

FEAR: **NOT TO BE FEARED** Every so often, in an article or an interview, someone describes me as "fearless." In my opinion, that's like calling me an idiot. Fear is a natural response. Without it, we wouldn't survive. If you're never scared, then you've either never been hurt or you're completely ignorant. The idea that fear is something to deny is completely misguided.

Forget your emotions around fear for a second and look at the simple reality: It's an energy source designed to increase performance. Adrenaline and the natural hormones your body creates when you're scared are more powerful than any drug. The ability to harness it constructively, that's the tricky part. Once you start to understand fear, it becomes something you can tap into. In my experience, fear usually prompts me to make really good decisions. I'd even go so far as to say that it gives me power.

How do you use fear to empower yourself? You don't fight it, and you don't overanalyze it. Thinking too much about a frightening situation causes your mind to start chattering, and it gets in the way of your body.

At Teahupoo, Tahiti, in 2000, I faced what has been, to date, the most dangerous situation of my career. I'd surfed this wave before, but never at the size it was that day—and neither had anybody else. The thing about Teahupoo is that it's a massively thick, deep, fast-moving barrel, and when it breaks it heaves so much water over the falls that it practically drains the reef. And the noise—you'd think it was a neutron bomb exploding. If you fall in the wrong conditions at Teahupoo, you're looking at a serious problem—possibly the last one you'll ever have.

When I let go of the rope after being towed in, I knew that the wave I'd just caught was a monster. But a split second later, I realized that it was actually a two-headed monster, unlike anything I'd ever ridden. My mind tried every trick in the book to get me to doubt my ability to survive what everyone could see (and I instinctively knew, even though it was behind me) was a potentially fatal ride. But if I had listened to those panicked thoughts and jumped off that wave, I probably wouldn't be here to tell you not to let panic dictate your actions.

If you think about it, the flip side of fear is commitment. You can spend your life fence-sitting because you're frightened of something bad that might happen—or you can launch yourself into it with all of your conviction and all of your intelligence. Here's my advice: Meet up with your fears. If you're afraid of sharks, go learn all about sharks. Get into the water with one. If you respect fear, face it straight on and act anyway. What you'll find isn't terror—it's exhilaration and the moments that you never forget.

NEGATIVITY: WE ALL GET IT, BUT THAT DOESN'T MEAN YOU HAVE TO TAKE IT

Negativity is going to crop up in your mind. I think that's an unfortunate part of being human. It's as sure as daytime, nighttime. The question is: How much life do you give it? How dominant do you let it get? You have to make sure that the positive has more power and gets more time in your head than the negative. If you let that negative side take charge, you're going to find yourself in a hole.

I can be as negative as anyone, but when it comes to what I'm doing in sports, that stuff is *out*. For instance, if I'm surfing and I start thinking about wiping out, that is getting pushed out of my brain. I'm consciously removing that thought; that's not something I'm giving any kind of life to. Mental discipline is key—and when it comes

DROPPING IN

GABBY REECE

I think I'm a pretty good athlete. I mean a good athlete. But it's a humbling thing being with someone like Laird. There are the 1 percent athletes—the people who are at the top of the college sports scene; the ones who become pros. About 1 percent of talented athletes will make it that far. But then, every so often, you get a Tiger Woods. He's like the 1 percent of the 1 percent—a different breed. And Laird is in that group. I've been around a lot of pro athletes, and I'll watch him training and think, *That's just a*

down to it, negativity is the easy way out. Quitting: easy. Daring to triumph: hard.

Your mind has 100 percent power over your reality. Whatever you believe, that's what you are cultivating. So if you're hurt and you're funneling all your energy into thinking *I'm getting better, I'm getting stronger*—then that's what will happen. At the same time, if you're thinking *Poor me. I'm wounded. I'm never going to be the same,* then you will end up with the fruits of those seeds.

If you're plagued by negative thoughts, here's a simple cure: Do something. If you think about it, negative thoughts are a luxury. They're a way to avoid getting down to work. We are each our own greatest inhibitors. We stop ourselves. The irony is that if you just get out of your own way, you'll do really well. And the sooner you face the work, the easier it'll be. The work will actually be the fun part.

whole other existence going on over there. Being around someone with that talent, whether it's in sports or art or science or whatever—you don't get in the way of it. You've got to support it because it's unique.

When we met, I knew exactly what Laird did for a living. As far as being nervous about it, I think I just accepted a long time ago that it's part of his destiny. You couldn't live with him if he wasn't doing it. It's all part of the deal. Over the years I've come to understand surfing and to appreciate how Laird approaches his sport. He has a lot of control and a lot of speed. His board is pushed into the wave rather than chattering across the face. Often he'll ride in a deeper position than other surfers, farther away from the shoulder, the wave's outside edge.

Even though the situations he's in can be radical and powerful, there's something straightforward about his arena. Nature isn't as capricious as humans are. The ocean lets you know up front: "I'm dangerous. And I'm coming from the north." It's consistent that way. I'm not going to say there aren't days when I say, "Hey, could you just call me when you get in? Please just check in with me." Because you do have those days.

CULTIVATING
INSTINCTS

SMELL, SIGHT, HEARING, TASTE, TOUCH—
DON'T FORGET YOUR SIXTH SENSE:
ANIMAL INSTINCT. NOT ONLY IS IT REAL,
IT CAN SAVE YOUR LIFE.

No matter what it was—whether someone was bitten by a shark, fell off a cliff, or anything—I'll bet 95 percent of the time anyone who's had something bad happen to them had a feeling right before. That prickly feeling on the back of your neck that says, "That's a dangerous spot." It's an intuition we've developed as a species because it's been necessary for survival over millions of years. And yet animal instinct isn't something we pay much attention to on a day-in, day-out basis. To a large extent, modern life has removed the necessity of being on our toes. The average person loses a lot of those signals.

I'm consciously aware of trying to cultivate my instincts. The less you react to them, the less you have them. They become numb. And I think most mistakes come when you don't pay attention to that inner knowledge. Ignore it and you end up going against your natural instincts. Learning to interpret what that sixth sense is telling you is as important as living and dying. I learned that the hard way.

Three years ago, I was heli-snowboarding in the Caucasus Mountains in Russia, between the Black Sea and the Caspian Sea. Little place called Sochi. I was with a group that included other snowboarders and some guides, and before we went out, we'd had this safety meeting about how to walk near cornices, which are always dangerous because they can collapse—and there's usually nothing beneath them but air. The guides stressed that if we saw stones (which can indicate an edge), we should always walk on the inside of them. But as we made our way along the steep traverse, the guides weren't doing that. I had a funny feeling, a sense something wasn't right, and I hollered at the guy in front of me. At the moment I yelled, I fell through a cornice, and due to nothing but luck, I landed on a rock shelf a few feet below. (Had that shelf not been there, I would have fallen 1,500 feet to my death.) And then I was thoroughly pissed. These guides were supposed to be getting me down safely. I was going down all right: the long way down, and the wrong way down.

When we're not operating in life-or-death situations, a lot of times we tune out. If you're sitting behind a desk all day, you don't have to be hyperaware. But it's important to exercise your instincts like you would a muscle. If you don't try to tune in to everything—smell, hearing, sight, vibration—you can get dull, and that might come back to haunt you when it matters most.

You can start by consciously turning your senses on. Be still, stay rooted in the present moment, and you'll start to become aware of all kinds of subtle things you hadn't noticed. Try to detect very faint smells. Or train your eyes to adjust more easily to the dark. The more you play with your senses, the more you're aware of them, the more you're in them. And the more you use them, the better you get.

15

THE JOY OF BEING A
BEGINNER

OR, WHY IT'S GOOD TO BE BAD.

In general, people don't want to try new things if they think they're going to be bad at them. The tendency is to say, "I haven't done that, I don't need to do that, I'm not good at that. You guys go on ahead."

But the truth is, you have to be willing to subject yourself to failure, to be bad at something, to fall on your butt and do it again, and try stuff you've never done. That's the ideal mind-set in sports and in life—you have to be willing to have people laugh at you at first.

Why? Because you need to keep challenging yourself. That's the whole idea behind seeking out things you're not good at: It forces your mind to engage. When you reach a certain level of proficiency in a sport or activity, your effort level is really diminished. Your body has adapted. For me personally, cross training—snowboarding, windsurfing, and mountain biking—keeps me physically and mentally sharp. Learning different sports always has a positive effect on my surfing. When you're a novice at something, it takes more focus and more concentration.

When you've got something mastered, it takes a lot for you to have fun, but when you're new at something, you have fewer expectations, so it's easier. Trying something for the first time, you may think you've just been out fumbling around for a few hours. But in truth, you've worked your brain, your nervous system—your entire body—more than you know.

Another advantage to beginner mind is that it keeps you humble. New things are always hard, of course, because you don't know what you're doing. Therefore, you don't

17

know what to anticipate. Your mind can't look at some program that it has already mapped out and been through a hundred times before.

Along with humility, you've got naïveté. And they're related: Humble is saying "I don't know," and naïveté is not knowing! To me, that's an important part of being a beginner—maintaining the ability to say, "Hi! I don't know how to do that." Think of children. Not knowing what you're doing is related to innocence, and that's part of being young. That's the bottom line: Trying new things keeps you perpetually young.

GOAL SETTING

FIVE STEPS TO GETTING WHERE YOU WANT TO GO

If you chart your destination, you have a better chance of arriving. Sure, every so often amazing things happen at random, but odds are you won't just wake up one morning to discover that you're the World Champion. If you have specific ambitions in mind, goal setting is mandatory. To translate your goals into reality, consider these five steps.

1. VISUALIZE Whatever you want to achieve, imagine it in every detail. When Michelangelo worked, he said that he could see the sculpture in the rock before he began to carve and that his job was merely to remove the excess stone. That's vision. Don't be afraid to really use your imagination. Let it run wild. It's one of the most powerful tools you've got.

For me, everything starts with visualizing. My goals are things I can see, whether it's a project, an idea, an invention, or anything else. I may have some new idea of how to ride a wave, for instance, and some underwater contraption (the hydrofoil surfboard, for instance) that I need to build in order to do it. But first I see it vividly in my mind's eye, and I know what I want. Envisioning things makes them tangible. When I was younger, I visualized myself becoming a father, a husband, and a good friend—I saw clearly the kind of man I wanted to be.

2. MAKE IT CHALLENGING When it comes to setting goals, I think people often underestimate themselves. Maybe it's human nature, and we're all suffering from a collective case of low self-esteem. The good news is that if you really put your mind to something, you can go a lot farther than you think. Few people on earth ever max out their full potential—but the most important thing is that you believe it about yourself. And if you don't believe you're capable of much, then guess what? You won't be.

So the trick is to strike a balance between setting goals that aren't too easy to obtain and goals that are completely impossible (because you don't want to set yourself up for failure, either). A goal that's a stretch, but *maybe* you could do it if you approached it right—that's the one to go for.

3. IMPROVISE ALONG THE WAY Once you've identified a goal, don't be rigid about how you're going to get there. Yes, the shortest distance between two points is a straight line, but life isn't like that (and it would be boring if it was). Sometimes

you have to go backward to get to a goal, or sideways, or around an impediment— the way a river flows around a mountain. You might even come to a dead stop. If that happens, the way to avoid frustration is to adapt. For instance, I'm constantly changing my schedule according to the weather. If there are no waves, it's hard to go surfing—but conditions might be perfect for swimming or cycling or building a fence. Point is, I'm still training, even though nature may have thrown me a curveball. So if things aren't going according to plan, take a fresh look at the plan. Don't be afraid to improvise if you need to. Or stay the course, give things more time, and adjust your expectations. Life doesn't necessarily obey the schedule you've come up with in your head.

4. ACCEPT THAT THERE WILL BE OBSTACLES Along the road to achieving your most ambitious goals, you have to expect the odd setback. It might take the form of resistance from people you encounter along the way, or maybe it'll be some situation that doesn't go as planned. This is the nature of aiming high—the route won't always be easy. For many people, the desire to avoid unpleasant realities is one of the strongest impulses in their life. My advice: Get over that. No one enjoys a struggle, but it's a necessary process.

Over the years, my biggest obstacles have been injuries—especially potentially career-ending ones. They're frustrating, inconvenient, unsettling, painful, and even frightening at times. But hating an injury won't make it heal faster; you have to start with acceptance. Face reality. And the irony is that when you do turn and face the problem, you'll get past it far easier than if you run away. Because it's just going to follow you. Avoiding something difficult now just means you're going to meet it again later.

5. ALLOW SATISFACTION (BUT KEEP YOUR EDGE) When you accomplish a goal, the passage from striving to achievement is an especially tricky one. If you're the kind of person who thrives on the process of making things happen, it's hard to sit back and relax when they do. Sometimes there can be a psychological down period after a highlight; I call it "post big-wave syndrome." In the beginning, before I understood it, it used to hammer me. It's a variation on depression, the flip side of an adrenaline high. I've heard people talk about feeling low in the aftermath of running a marathon they'd spent months training for or after winning a major award in their profession. My friend Eddie Vedder (from Pearl Jam) told me that he sometimes feels that letdown after a big show. At the moment when you should be enjoying your achievement, you feel completely deflated instead.

It's worth making an effort to savor what you've just done. Instead of rushing on to a newer, harder goal, let yourself enjoy a moment of satisfaction. The next big thing isn't going anywhere. You'll be at it soon enough.

Part of a ride/paddle we did across approximately 483 miles of Hawaiian Islands for autism awareness.

ON EXCELLENCE

I'VE BEEN FORTUNATE TO HAVE SPENT TIME WITH GREAT ATHLETES FROM MANY SPORTS, TO HAVE TRAINED WITH THEM AND TRADED IDEAS WITH THEM. PEOPLE ASK, "WHAT IS IT ABOUT THE BEST ATHLETES THAT MAKES THEM SEEM INVINCIBLE? IS IT PHYSICAL? PSYCHOLOGICAL? GENETIC?" AND MY ANSWER TO THAT IS: YES TO ALL OF THE ABOVE. IF YOU CAN CHECK OFF THE LIST ON THE FOLLOWING PAGES, YOU'RE BUILDING A CHAMPION'S RÉSUMÉ.

BEING THE BEST

✥ **YOU'VE GOT CERTAIN BASIC STRENGTHS** *Some things have to be there from the start; they can't be learned, they can't be trained. Sorry to say, you can't make an eagle out of a chicken. As Gabby's volleyball coach said once, "You can't train height." And it goes beyond the physical. You can't train courage, either. You might be able to enhance the courage you already have, but if you have a fearful mind, that's always going to work against you. Self-doubt is as good as kryptonite.*

The best athletes have a huge tolerance for work. You have to ask yourself, How much work do I want to do? What's my work capacity? Certain people have a 10-gallon tank no matter what. They don't have a 25-gallon tank. I have a theory that that's established when you're young: How you grew up—and what you did during your growth stages— determines your work capacity. And then genetics, psychology, and probably a couple of other things play into that. But by the time you're a young adult, I believe, your work capacity is pretty set. If you sat around eating cereal, watching TV, and playing video games from age 6 to 16—you're shot. Your body has developed its whole working system. Now, if since you were a little kid, you ran around all day long, doing all this cardio activity—you're going to have a big tank. If you're highly active as you're growing, your body's going to grow differently.

✥ **DISTRACTIONS DON'T PHASE YOU** *Sticks and stones, whatever. If you want to be the best, you can't be distracted. Or, to put it another way, if there are distractions (and there always will be), they don't matter. When I'm surfing, people drop in on me; they'll trash-talk, they'll do stupid things that endanger themselves and those around* *them. But when you're really in the moment, those unexpected pressures, clashes with others, or adverse situations—they don't phase you. You might even figure out a way to use them to your benefit. If there's a lot of chaos going on, it forces you to focus on exactly what you're doing, and, therefore, you're less likely to overthink things. Anything that impedes your full concentration will have to wait for later.*

YOU'RE TOUGH *Mental and physical toughness are both important. You may have more of one than the other, but the bottom line is: You don't cave in. There are people whose bodies aren't superior genetically, but their minds allow them to deal with extreme amounts of pain. So many of us are capable of so much more than we think. The toughest athletes push that threshold so far out that they redefine what's humanly possible. Look at my friend Chris Chelios, the Detroit Red Wings defenseman. He just won another Stanley Cup—at age 46. And when you watch him train for 6 hours a day, you understand why he's still a champion long after other guys would've retired. I've said this before, but here it is again: I don't care what kind of natural talents you have; you still have to do the work.*

YOU'RE SENSITIVE TO EVERYTHING AROUND YOU *We've all seen clueless people: out of touch with their surroundings; oblivious to what's at stake or what's really going on. Ignorance can definitely be bliss, but it doesn't ever add up to greatness. When you're sensitive, it means you're aware of everything that's happening around you—little details that others would miss. You're awake. That alone makes you more intelligent at whatever you're doing.*

✤ YOU SWEAT THE DETAILS *I think this is a corollary of being sensitive. If you care about what you're doing and you're aware of every part of it, then you're not satisfied with subpar execution. Of anything. You're going to make a point of being technically immaculate. Your equipment will be maintained to perfection. You'll practice your weaknesses until you don't have any. You're going to be out there on the worst, coldest, ugliest days doing whatever needs to be done. Half-assed is not part of your mind-set. The more that's at stake, the more prepared you will be.*

✤ YOU DON'T INDULGE THE VOICE OF DOUBT *We all hear that negative voice inside our heads, but that doesn't mean we have to indulge it. Just because it's there, it doesn't have to have an effect. Once again, you decide what you want to believe. Is the cup half full or half empty? Do you believe you're going to stick the mountain bike downhill— or fall on your head? Success or failure, determination or uncertainty; these aren't externally determined things. They're personal choices.*

✤ YOU CAN OPERATE HURT *Who can forget watching Michael Jordan hit a play-off-winning three-pointer at the buzzer while sweating out a 103-degree fever? He was so sick, his skin looked purple. Ironically, some great performances can happen when you're hurt, sick, or injured. Why? Because you don't have any energy to waste. You have to perform more efficiently and more precisely. I know that* personally. I've done some of my best surfing injured. I can remember surfing Pipeline with a cast on my ankle. Every nerve ending was firing; I was so aware of the pain. I really didn't want to fall, so every move I made was precise. Sometimes when you're hurt you have to stay home. But sometimes you can transcend it. When the subconscious part of your brain kicks in—the part that's operating out of necessity rather than desire—you're in a more efficient and more powerful frame of mind.

❖ YOU'RE SOLID In the biggest sense, it's about you, the whole person. There's a depth of character that underlies all great performances, and it all comes down to this question: Who are you? Are you someone who cares about others, who'll notice someone struggling and stop what you're doing to go over and help? Are you a person of principle—or a creature of opportunity? Are you honest, or will you do anything to win? If you cut corners in your integrity, it doesn't matter how many trophies you've got stuffed into your case.

THE BRAIN

MIND **YOUR** *MIND* In the same way a great conductor can take a dozen musicians and turn their different melodies into one beautiful song, the brain orchestrates the body. Much of the time in sports, the emphasis is on the physical: how to make your body stronger, faster, more resilient. And yet it's the brain that tells the muscles what to do. It operates all your processes, all your hormone levels, all your impulses—everything. If the brain says "Go!" you're going.

On the flip side, if you're neurologically exhausted, it doesn't matter how physically capable you are. When your brain doesn't have proper fuel, that's when you'll bonk. Your muscles and your brain both require glycogen (made from glucose, a simple sugar that results from carbohydrates) to make energy. If there isn't enough to go around, muscles can burn fat as an alternative energy source. The brain can't. Evolution has set it up so that the brain gets first dibs.

And the body serves the brain in other ways, too. After all, it's carrying it and giving it blood. Physical exertion causes the brain to grow new nerve cells and prevents memory decline and other cognitive disorders. Various scientific studies have shown that inactive people are twice as likely to develop Alzheimer's. I have a theory that many people have undernourished brains. They're not healthy because they're not pumping enough blood through their systems to make everything function properly. In our biological past, movement wasn't optional. There was hunting and gathering to be done. People moved from place to place by foot. Any of our ancestors who sat around the cave all day—the way so many people now sit in front of the television or computer screen—wouldn't have survived. When you exercise, you're pumping blood to your brain and feeding it with oxygen, among other things. You have to feed it so that it will feed you.

Think of your body as a vehicle (which it is—without it, how would you get anywhere?). First, you want the machinery to work. You want big pistons. Nice shocks. But all of that isn't enough. None of it will do you any good if it's lying in a pile in the corner. It also needs the right fuel; timely maintenance; and, of course, a driver. That's where your brain comes in. Often, when people think about fitness, they think of muscles and body fat measurements and how they look in front of a mirror. And those things aren't insignificant, but I'd still argue that the most important factor in your overall health is the engine that's running between your ears.

PART 2

B O D Y

I look at my athletic career as the intersection of two lines on a graph. One line shows my physical abilities, such as oxygen uptake and muscle density, either flattening or gradually declining. The other line shows the cerebral factors—maturity, judgment, experience, passion, perspective—continually rising. Where the two lines cross, I regard that place as my peak. Which is to say that my body's performance isn't only reflective of the motor or the pistons or the shocks but also of my enthusiasm and accrued skill, whether I can continue to surprise myself. To me, conventional wisdom about fitness is an oxymoron. Let's break the mold instead.

TRAINING

I don't have a set routine. To my mind, that's the quickest route to burnout (and it's deeply unimaginative besides). To be healthy, to sleep well, to eat well: These things are essential every day. Over the years I've discovered what works for me—and what doesn't. Those strategies, which follow, are interwoven into whatever I'm doing.

My activities vary daily, weekly, seasonally, geographically, psychologically, depending on who's in town—you name it. The best way to maximize what a day has to offer is to look outside your window that morning, and then look inside yourself. What are the conditions? What are your options? What are your goals? What do you feel like doing? What does your body need? What did you do yesterday? Those are the variables. Consider them all, and come up with a plan.

Fitness doesn't have to be a duty. It doesn't have to mean charts and graphs and heart rate printouts. It should be a pleasurable part of your life, and it should include things that you do purely because you enjoy them. Fun is an ingredient that people often forget in their fitness program. Put your imagination to work on your daily routine, and watch things change for the better.

TRAINING INTELLIGENCE

My routine, which is more like an antiroutine, changes depending on the conditions. If the surf's perfect, you're not going to find me in the gym. Having variety in your training matters because it keeps things interesting for your brain and your body. No matter what I'm doing on a given day, it's based on these strategies.

⇕ **BUILD FUNCTIONAL FITNESS** It's not how much weight you can lift, it's how much strength you can incorporate into your movements. You want strength that you can actually control and apply. Take big wave surfing, which requires tremendous leg strength. There are guys who are stronger than I am. Physically, they can squat more—but are they able to apply all that power into the edge of the board and project it into the right part of the wave? The ability to put all of your resources to work—that's the real trick.

When you sit down on a piece of exercise equipment, you tend to shut down the rest of your body. You might isolate your biceps or your chest, but in reality, that's not how you use your strength. If I'm working on a machine, I'll add movements so the other muscles aren't static. I might incorporate leg lifts while I'm doing chest presses or do my shoulder presses while balancing. When you're performing a motion, try to recruit more than one muscle group.

⇕ **BE CREATIVE** Do the same workout every day and you'll get consistent—but you won't get explosive. Once you become too efficient at something, it benefits you less. I believe in keeping the body guessing. One way to do that is to let the conditions dictate what you do. If it's windy, instead of going to the gym, you might go windsurfing—or even run around outside and fly a kite. If you're at the gym, don't just repeat the same routine every time. Change it up. Try it back-to-front, or work only on machines that you've never used before. Make it new, not just for your body, but also for your brain.

WORK YOUR BALANCE The best way I've found to cultivate balance is standup paddling (see page 203), but you can incorporate balance work into anything you're doing. Look for balance boards in the gym, or simply lift one foot off the ground while you're doing biceps curls or other arm exercises. Working balance on both sides of your body helps in all sports—we all have one side that's dominant. To really excel at something, you need to shore up your weak side so that you really don't have a weak side.

DON'T TRAIN FOR WHAT YOU DON'T WANT TO HAPPEN You can teach your body bad habits as well as good ones. And when your body learns, so does your mind. In fact, they don't just learn, they memorize—and they do so especially well under duress. In surfing, I'll see guys training, and they'll say, "I can hold my breath for 5 minutes underwater with a rock!" Well, great. Personally, I don't ever want to consciously inform myself that I could hold my breath for that long because I believe that if you cultivate the idea, there's a good chance you're going to bring on the occasion. People ask me all the time, "How long can you hold your breath?" and I say, "I don't want to know how long. I just know so far, long enough!"

◈ **PRACTICE BREATH AWARENESS** Even though I don't want to work on breath holding, I think it's good to practice deep breathing. After all, breathing is our only form of nutrition besides food. It oxygenates the blood, tissues, and entire body. Taking shallow breaths all the time is like watering down your own scotch. The other thing about breath awareness is that it's calming. Whenever you think about breathing, rather than letting it happen as an unconscious reflex, you bring yourself into the present moment. And there aren't a lot of distractions there, so it's a great place to find clarity and peacefulness. For a quality breath, inhale deeply, expanding your stomach from the diaphragm outward. When you exhale, contract your stomach. (Often, people do this in reverse.)

◈ **LEAN INTO THE WORK** Certain people have a gift for hand-eye coordination or generating speed or building muscle, and once they learn how to apply those skills, they're naturals. But that doesn't mean they don't also have to work. At the end of the day, if you're talented, great—but it's still all about the work. One of the main purposes of training is to build confidence, to put yourself through extraordinary paces so that nothing catches you unprepared. I don't want to be going over the falls at Teahupoo about to have my face ripped off on the reef, thinking, *I could have done with a few more squats*. Rather than resisting hard work, embrace it.

◈ **MAKE IT FUN** Let's be realistic; you're not going to work out like a maniac and be in peak shape in a week. Real fitness happens over time. Try to enjoy what you're doing— and if you can't, if working out is a big grind for you, then reevaluate what you're up to. When you see people slogging it out on the elliptical trainer every day, none of them looks like they're really into it. They have to watch TV just to keep their minds off what they're doing. That might help you pass the time, but it won't do much for your fitness. Design your routines to include activities that you love.

THE BUILDING BLOCKS OF SPORT

ALL SPORTS RELY ON THESE BASIC INGREDIENTS. HERE'S HOW TO GET THE RIGHT MIX.

SPEED In my sport, speedwork isn't about generating speed with my body, it's about training myself to perform at high speeds: sharpening my reflexes, instincts, and hand-eye coordination. Doing anything fast requires making split-second decisions, many of which aren't even conscious. They're impulses that your body processes on a deeper level. Think of a computer doing its calculations before spitting out information—it happens in a nanosecond, so far in the background that you're barely aware of it. But somebody programmed the computer first so it would be up to the job. It's the same thing in the athletic world. To perform at top speed, you need to train your body to make intelligent, efficient decisions with less response time.

Anything that increases your ability to react will help you handle speed. And in sports, velocity is your friend—it can get you out of potentially dangerous situations. Downhill ski racers, who routinely hit 70 miles per hour (mph) on the mountain, work their reflexes using video games and cross-train in Formula 1 race cars. If you're used to dealing with 100 mph, then 70 mph will seem slow. On big waves I'm moving somewhere in the neighborhood of 50 mph, with bumps and other obstacles rearing up in front of me.

Whatever you're doing at high speed becomes exaggerated. Rough things get rougher. Your weaknesses get magnified. That's why you want to make sure that your foundation's in place before you open the throttle.

I train my reflexes by doing speed runs on a Jet Ski in rough water, downhill mountain biking, backcountry snowboarding, and performance driving. And recently I started helicopter-flying lessons—the ultimate reaction test because you can move in every dimension and every direction. Short of having an aircraft or a race car in your garage, the simulations at the video arcade are a good place to start.

STRENGTH In theory, it's a simple formula: To build strength, increase resistance. In practice, things are more complicated. For instance, timing is important. If your training's geared toward heavier lifting, you must be disciplined about your schedule. You're tearing the muscles down, so you need to allow recovery time before you stress them again. It's best to divide your workouts by body part— focus on your chest and arms today, switch to your legs and back tomorrow. Otherwise, you'll build endurance but you won't increase strength.

Diet also plays a key role here. Consider raising your protein intake so that your body has what it needs to generate the amino acids that will build new muscles and help existing muscles recover. One protein powder that I like is Muscle Milk (see page 115). It has an impressive blend of ingredients, is easy to digest, and isn't packed with sugar. Drinking a protein shake before or after a hard workout is a good idea. If you want a bigger engine, you've got to fuel it right.

Another thing to keep in mind when building muscle is that extra mass will take a toll on your endurance level. Every 5 pounds is going to cut into your stamina because you're carrying it around, and it takes more energy to sustain it. In many sports (including the ones I do), bulk isn't an asset. Depending on your activities of choice, you might not want to make building muscle mass your first priority. And even if you do, it's important to make sure that you're building functional power and not just an impressive physique. The last thing you want is to gain strength and lose range of motion. It helps to work with a good trainer who can tailor a program to your athletic goals.

ENDURANCE Endurance is easy to define: It's the ability to keep going; to do something continuously under a moderate load for a sustained period of time. But that doesn't mean it's easy, period. There's definitely a mental aspect to building endurance. You know you're on the right track when you hear the voice in your head say *I want to stop— now.* Push past that and you'll find a deep calm that settles in after a long workout, when you've exhausted yourself. I like that feeling.

If you want to increase endurance, first you need to understand your body's threshold. How much energy can you put out, and how long can you keep it up? Once you have that information, then you can build on it. But you can't start to push past your edge until you know where it is.

How do you figure this out? You learn to feel it so that it becomes instinctive. You go out and discover how fast, how long, and how hard you can do something before your system over-revs. Ignore the charts and graphs about heart rates. I can't buy that everyone who's 70 is the same or that all 40-year-olds should be doing X . . . according to whom? That's like saying every car is a 1972 Buick Skylark. I don't think you can generalize. Every individual's aerobic threshold (or VO_2 max, your maximum ability to transport and use oxygen during exercise) arrives at a different speed, after a different duration, and at a different heart rate. If you want to use a heart rate monitor, they do work. Personally, I don't because I want to use my own intelligence about my own body.

Gears on a bicycle (or the power output on a stationary bike) will give you a good baseline. If you can pedal for 15 minutes in a certain gear before coming apart, then next time try it for 20 minutes. When you're trying to expand your aerobic fitness, consistency and tenacity are key.

Another method of endurance training is to challenge yourself to go from point A to point B. No matter how you get there—pedaling, paddling, walking, running, swimming—set it up so that it will take you some time. Recently, I've been paddling across channels, including the English Channel (see page 216). Next I'm planning a crossing of the Bering Strait. As far as building endurance goes, nothing I've ever done has worked better than this. So chart yourself a journey. You'll build endurance. You'll have a target to focus on. And you'll accomplish something far greater than a gym workout.

THE *CIRCUIT*

During the summer, when I come back to California from Hawaii, I train in the gym more than I do at any other time of the year. A group of us meet in the mornings at our friend Don Wildman's (see page 162) gym in Malibu, and we spend 2 to 3 hours doing a workout that we call the Circuit. More than a specific workout, the Circuit is a strategy for working out—one that I believe is the single best approach for training in the gym. Here's why: On your next visit to the health club, notice how much time people spend sitting around between sets. Not only does all this rest decrease the intensity of your training, it means that your workout will take forever! And if you're logging all this time hanging around the gym getting mediocre results, eventually you're going to become unmotivated and burned out. The Circuit enables you to dial up your intensity while keeping yourself stimulated. If you apply yourself to this method of training, you'll get much greater results in half the time.

THE IDEA On the pages that follow, I've outlined a group of 15 exercises that resembles the Circuit we do in Malibu. Once you understand the basics behind this kind of workout, you'll have a formula for training with whatever equipment's on hand. Even if you only have a pair of dumbbells, you can create a routine that works your entire body. And if you're in a fully outfitted gym, you can adapt the Circuit endlessly so that you'll never become bored. It all works if you keep these fundamentals in mind.

KEEP MOVING The Circuit is all about continual motion; you want to get your heart rate up so you're getting a cardio workout while you're lifting. That means moving from

47

exercise to exercise with as little downtime as possible. The key to being able to do this is to strategically plan the order in which you perform the exercises.

✥ **ALTERNATE BETWEEN MUSCLE GROUPS** If you do three exercises in a row that all work your quadriceps muscles, you'll get tired fast and have to stop. Which is why, in the Circuit, you'll alternate between muscle groups on each exercise. After an upper-body exercise, for instance, the next move might be for your lower body. You can also alternate between opposing muscle groups such as biceps/triceps, quadriceps/hamstrings, or chest/back. That way, you can maintain a higher level of intensity. You'll be pumping blood up and down your body throughout the workout and minimizing your need for rest.

✥ **USE YOUR CORE** During the Circuit, you want to engage your core whenever possible, particularly when you're using a machine that isolates a certain body part. Machines are great at targeting a specific area, but that's not the way we use our strength in real life. When I'm on a seated machine, rather than letting the rest of my body shut down, I try to also incorporate core work into the exercise. It could be as simple as keeping my midsection tight throughout the movement. Or I might perform the move while standing on an unstable surface (which forces you to engage your core), such as an inverted Bosu ball or a balance board or while balancing on one leg.*

✥ **WRITE YOUR WORKOUT IN PENCIL AND ERASE OFTEN** You'll get far more out of your workouts if you vary them often rather than repeating the same routine over and

---

*All of the exercises that call for standing on an inverted Bosu ball can also be done standing on the ground. Before increasing the degree of difficulty on any movement, make sure that your form is perfect. If you're not sure about any movement, enlist a trainer to critique your form. If your technique's off, nothing you do in your training will really work that well. Also, practicing bad form is a good way to get injured.

over. Changing things up keeps your body on its toes and prevents you from becoming too complacent. There are many ways to shake things up. You might switch the order and do the Circuit from back to front; you might decide one day only to use machines that you've never used before. The next day you could try using only dumbbells. You also need to consider the layout of the gym when planning your Circuit so that it flows optimally. If the chest machines are located a football field away from the back machines, take that into account. Always make sure you can move efficiently from one exercise to the next.

✥ **KNOW WHERE YOUR EDGES ARE AND GET CLOSE TO THEM** Ideally, during every workout, you'd max out your muscles so that on your last rep of the day, you were totally spent. In practice, that's pretty hard to do. However, you do want to make sure that you adjust the weights according to your ability. If it's easy to complete a set, then increase weight incrementally. It should be difficult but not impossible to finish your reps. This is especially important on a short set, where you're doing only 5 reps. Those 5 reps need to be high quality. If you get to 5 easily, add a few more reps and increase your weight next time.

✥ **HAVE A CARDIO CHASER** When we do the Circuit at Don's, we follow it with an hour-long mountain bike ride to help flush the lactic acid out of our muscles. Whenever you're lifting hard, it helps to finish your workout with at least 15 to 30 minutes of riding, running, rowing, swimming—any activity that gets your body moving. You don't have to go hard, but the movement itself will help with recovery.

THREE WAYS
TO DO THE CIRCUIT

Depending on how hard you want to go and how much time you have, you can choose how many rounds you want to do and how many reps you'll do in each round.

1. THE BASIC CIRCUIT Three rounds: First round is 25 reps; second round is 15; third round is 5. Increase weight on each round (one rule of thumb is that the fewer reps you're doing, the heavier you want to go). Always choose your weights so that it's difficult but not impossible to complete the reps. **Takes:** 1+ hour

2. THE ONE-ROUND ENDURANCE CIRCUIT One round: Do 40 to 60 reps (as many as you can do, keeping good form) of each exercise with light weights. **Takes:** 1 hour

3. THE GRIND Six rounds: First round is 30 reps; second round is 20; third round is 10; fourth round is 5 (as heavy as you can go); fifth round is 15; sixth round is 25. Increase weight progressively on the first four rounds as the reps decrease. On the fifth and sixth sets, use whatever weight you need to use to complete the reps. This is the progression that we use most often in Malibu. It's a lot of lifting, but you'll enjoy a real feeling of accomplishment when you finish it. **Takes:** 2+ hours

1. CRUNCH

Note: Crunches have a different rep count.

For: your abdominal muscles and obliques (the muscles along your sides that enable you to bend and twist)

You'll do 90 crunches total. The first 30 are done lying on your back; then do 30 on each side. Clasp your hands behind your head, look toward the ceiling, and contract your abs to raise your shoulders and upper back off the ground. Make sure you don't pull on your head or neck with your hands and that your elbows remain aligned with your ears.

2. PLANK

For: your abdominal muscles and glutes

Arms are bent at a 90-degree angle with elbows directly under your shoulders and palms flat on the ground, directly under shoulders. Hold for 1 minute.

3. CABLE PULLDOWN

For: your back, especially the large latissimus dorsi muscles, and shoulders

Use an overhand grip with your hands slightly more than shoulder-width apart, and pull the cables (or bar) down. Keep your body stationary; make sure you're not rocking backward and using that momentum to move the weight.

4. CHEST PRESS

For: your pectoral muscles, or chest

There are all kinds of ways to do a chest press, both on a machine and with free weights on a bench. If you use the latter, you can vary the movement by changing the position of your body: flat, decline, or incline. Each angle works your chest slightly differently: Lifting on an incline works higher up on your pectorals; on a decline, you'll stress the lower area more. If you bench-press lying flat, you bring your shoulders into the movement more than you would on an incline or a decline.

5. LEG EXTENSION

For: your quadriceps, the large group of muscles in your thighs, and the muscle above your knee (the vastus medialis)

Sitting with your back flat and your feet hooked behind the pads, straighten your legs (being careful not to lock or hyperextend your knees). Slowly lower legs to starting position.

6. DEAD LIFT

For: the group of muscles that run down the back of your thighs

Grab the bar with an overhand grip, keeping your arms straight and back flat. Stand up, lifting bar to the tops of your thighs.

7. SCARECROW ON BOSU BALL

Note: This exercise has a different rep count.

For: the group of four muscles and several tendons that stabilize your shoulder joint

The key to doing this movement is that you never want to use heavy weights. So on each round of the Circuit, do 20 reps of this exercise with light weights. To add some challenge, do it while standing on an unstable surface. I use an inverted Bosu ball.

Begin by standing, holding a pair of light free weights, palms facing down. Lift your arms laterally so your hands are at shoulder level, then bend your elbows to a 90-degree angle, as though you're about to do a shoulder press. But instead of pressing the weights above your head, rotate your hands 90 degrees downward, as though closing a window. Then raise them back up to complete the movement. Make sure your elbows remain stationary, so that your hands and lower arms are basically pivoting around them.

8. BICEPS CURL

For: the "flexing muscles" on the inside of your upper arms

If you're using dumbbells, alternate your arms. This is another exercise that's great to do on an inverted Bosu ball or some other unstable surface. Contracing biceps, pull weight toward your shoulder. Be careful to keep your elbows close to your body.

9. TRICEPS KICKBACK

For: the muscles on the back of your upper arms

Holding the weight in one hand, place your other hand and leg on a bench with your back straight and other leg on the floor. Lift your arm up, tucking to your side. Extend the dumbbell back until your arm is parallel to the floor.

10. SQUAT

For: all the muscles in your legs and buttocks and your lower back

Stand with your feet hip-width apart, with a barbell across the back of your shoulders and neck. Your knees are slightly bent, your back is straight, and your eyes are focused directly in front of you. Squat down as deeply as you can, while keeping your back straight and your feet flat on the ground. Your weight should be largely on your heels. Straighten your legs to complete the movement. Make sure to keep your core firm throughout the exercise to help support your back and that your knees never go beyond your toes.

11. SHOULDER PRESS

For: your deltoids, the biggest muscles in your shoulders

Holding dumbbells at your sides, palms facing forward, sit facing forward on a straight-backed bench. Bring the dumbbells to shoulder level. Straighten your arms to press the weights overhead.

12. CHEST FLY

For: your pectoral muscles

Holding dumbbells, lie on an adjustable bench seat at a decline. Bring the dumbbells straight above your shoulders with your palms facing each other. Keeping a slight bend in your elbows, open your arms to the side.

13. SITUP ON STABILITY BALL

For: your abdominal muscles

Sit on the edge of a large stability ball. Lean back with your feet flat on the floor. Place your hands behind your head and crunch upward. If you want to make this more difficult, you can hold a weight behind your head (but make sure you're not pulling on your neck).

14. LOW ROW

For: your upper and middle back and the backs of your
shoulders

Sit in front of a cable row with your legs slightly bent. Gripping
the handles, contract your shoulder blades and pull the
handles toward you. Keep your elbows close to your body.
Make sure that your back doesn't hunch on this one.

15. UPRIGHT ROW ON BOSU BALL

For: your shoulders, upper back, and arms

Stand on the Bosu ball, facing straight ahead, holding the weights with your palms facing you. Slowly lift by
bending your elbows and raising them toward your shoulders. The weights should stop at the same level as
your collarbone.

DROPPING IN

T. R. GOODMAN

T. R. Goodman is an expert trainer who works with athletes from the NFL, NHL, and other sports, as well as martial arts specialists, from his base at Gold's Gym in Venice, California. Gabby introduced me to T. R. several years ago; she and my friend (Detroit Red Wings defenseman) Chris Chelios were both training with him, and I joined them. T. R.'s philosophy is that you build athletic strength from the ground up. We all carry stresses in our bodies, though most of the time we're not consciously aware of them. T. R. begins by correcting those underlying problems, and then he adds on layers of intensity. Here, he explains his Pro Camp process.

- I've been in the fitness business since 1983, and during that time I've seen every crazy fitness theory to come along. For the past 25 years, I've been developing a training process that allows people to perform at a high level and to sustain that level without breaking down. My job is to get their bodies rejuvenated so they can perform optimally.
- When I first started training people, I thought

T. R. Goodman and Chris Chelios

if I could reduce their body fat—you know, make them look better—they would automatically become better athletes. Or if I could get someone to go from lifting 100 pounds to lifting 150, that would be success. But I've learned that cosmetic appearance or how much weight someone can lift is only a small part of performance. After all, if you're hurt and you're in the stands watching, none of the other stuff matters. I had to come up with a way to make sure that an athlete's increased intensity wouldn't lead to injury. So then my training method changed.

✤ Now my underlying philosophy is to fortify the body. My method is high intensity with low impact. It begins by removing the ingrained trauma from the body and strengthening the internal structure.

✤ Sports require repetitive movements. But when you do a motion over and over, your body starts to compensate, favoring certain muscles and shutting others off. Over time, that pattern becomes trapped in your body. Some parts become overworked; others, underworked. That's what we mean by trauma—and you've been accumu-

lating it since infancy.

✤ Some of the trauma comes in structural form, in your body's alignment. Some of it resides in the muscle tissue itself; we might work that out with massage. Some traumas might not respond to one type of soft tissue treatment, but they will to another.

✤ One big mistake athletes make is to try to get stronger before they've eliminated these compensations. Here's an example of what I mean by compensation: Take a mountain bike rider. That sport puts a lot of wear and tear on the hip flexors. And then the psoas (a thick internal muscle that stabilizes the base of the spine) gets tight and pulls the hips forward. And then your hamstrings get tight because your hips are pulled forward. So then you're walking around thinking, *My hamstrings are tight; I've got to stretch them.* But the reason you're tight is structural, so stretching your hamstrings is the worst thing you can do—they're already pulled to the max! All you're doing is causing more damage.

✤ Or let's say I sit in an office all day. What happens? My shoulders get rounded forward. My chest gets short

(*continued*)

and tight. And then what do I do? I walk into the gym and head straight for the bench press. But my chest is already short and tight from sitting in front of the computer for 10 hours. If I work it, that just makes it tighter, and the next thing I know, I've got problems in my neck and my lower back. You have to make sure the shoulders are sitting optimally before you work the chest.

❖ This level of awareness is where fitness has to go in the future. Generally, it's not part of the fitness business now.

❖ Core strength is key to successful training. Now, most people think of their abdominal muscles as their "core." Which is true, but you have two sets of abs: You have an external set and an internal set. One lies over top of the other. The bottom set holds the skeletal system together and maintains proper postural alignment. The top set includes the bigger, more explosive muscles. Likewise, your spine has a core, your shoulders have a core, and your hips have a core.

❖ Most of the time when people do abdominal exercises, they're working their hip flexors way too much. If you hook your feet at the top of a decline bench and do a situp, that's a ton of strain on your hip flexors.

❖ When there are deficiencies in core strength (in any area) or poor skeletal alignment, that shows up as inefficiencies in your movement. Your body fights itself.

❖ You watch people running, and a lot of the time it looks like they're in pain. Maybe that's not the best exercise for them at that point in their athletic development. Be aware of what's going on with your body. Don't force it to compensate as you train.

❖ After we strengthen the core, we work muscular endurance. No matter what sport you do, there's a repetitive element to it. So you need to be able to perform a movement over and over without losing control. Always increase reps (stamina) before you increase weight strength.

❖ There's a difference between muscular endurance and cardiovascular endurance, though the two are interrelated. Think of a hybrid car—

your body works in a similar way. Cardiovascular endurance uses one source of energy, and muscular endurance uses another.

- After endurance, then we build strength. And only then will we move to high-intensity work. But even that is low impact. We do explosive plyometric movements, but we do them in a way that's not jarring.
- Exercise execution is critical. Use a consistently controlled rep speed through a full range of motion in both directions. Don't rush it. Controlling rep speed forces every bit of your muscle fiber to fight the heaviness of the weight. When the weight is moving toward your body, that improves deceleration; away from your body improves acceleration.
- I believe that Laird is the best athlete in the world, hands down. He has the ability to generate a high level of intensity and maintain it. Many great athletes can do that but not to the degree he does. In his element, he's dealing with life and death.
- I try to come up with exercises that push him. I'll put him on a balance board barefoot and have him squat 275 pounds. Things like that.
- Most pro athletes need to remember to keep things in balance. Many of these guys are just yang, yang, yang. So then when they get injured, it's catastrophic. They'll blow out an ankle or a knee.
- Laird has the mental and physical ability to adapt to any sport. I think you could put him on a bike and he would finish the Tour de France. Okay, he might not win, but he would finish. The first time he went on a street luge, it was headfirst at 65 miles per hour. His body knows how to react to speed. In terms of strength, if he had been born anywhere else, he might have been a shortstop or a linebacker. I think he's too aggressive to have been a quarterback.

BUILDING LEG STRENGTH

The best way I can imagine to develop lower-body strength would be to take standard training moves like lunges and, instead of performing them on solid ground, do them in wet concrete. I'm not really suggesting that you head to a construction site—other types of unstable, resistance-offering environments can provide the same benefits. To start, find a beach that has deep, soft sand that your feet will sink into, and run. In Malibu, where I train during the summer, I run up and down the sand dunes near my house, carrying my daughter Reece on my back.

For legs, I also like the concept of towing things. Build yourself a harness and drag a heavy log behind you. (The movement will engage your core and shoulders as well.) Along with soft sand, water's great because it, too, offers resistance. Move fast through the shallow water along the shoreline, towing your kid behind you on a boogie board, and tell me you're not winded. And if you find yourself in a place with plenty of snow, put on some boots and go marching around. Plowing through snowdrifts forces you to lift your feet high under heavy resistance, while your body works overtime to maintain its core temperature in the cold. I think of deep snow as one of the greatest training opportunities in the world.

The other part of this strategy is that topographically uneven ground works your entire lower half, not just specialized muscles like your quadriceps or glutes. Often when people talk about leg strength, they're not thinking holistically. To me, it's about working every last part of your foundation: feet, toes, ankles, even your arches. The smaller muscles need more time and attention because they're the first to tire. You can have the gnarliest legs of all time, but if your toes don't hold an edge, you're stuck. If your ankles buckle, you're not going anywhere.

GOING BAREFOOT

Here's one simple way to benefit your legs (and the rest of your body): Take off your shoes.

Sports stores are filled with high-tech running shoes. They're designed to cushion impact, stabilize feet, support ankles—they'll practically go running for you. But your foot's natural range of motion is complex. Putting it on a fixed platform, such as a shoe, is like strapping a two-by-four to your leg. As many runners are discovering, shoes can actually decondition feet. That weakness leads to decreased performance and increased injury, which is why many athletes are now incorporating barefoot training into their workouts.

I go barefoot whenever I can. When I surf, I'm using every last muscle, ligament, and tendon down there. There's a matrix of tiny muscles between the sole and ankle that most people aren't even aware of. I need them. I need my feet and toes to be able to dig in; to be sensitive, flexible, strong, and resilient. I don't need them to be trussed up and immobile—ever.

And I have another reason for losing the shoes. During any given second, somewhere on earth, lightning strikes the ground about 100 times. That's 6,000 bolts per minute, each delivering a massive jolt of energy (lightning can deliver more voltage than the sun). The ground is charged, and I want to feel that. Eastern medicine has long advanced the art of reflexology, where the soles of the feet are considered to be the body's energy conductors. Many scientists and healers believe this connection is critical; after all, our cardiovascular and nervous systems function through electrical impulses. It doesn't matter whether you believe this or if it's been given the official nod by science. Anyone who's ever walked barefoot through warm sand or cool grass knows that feeling the earth through your soles is one of life's great joys.

THE ANYWHERE
WORKOUT

You don't need a gym. And on a beautiful day, why would you even want one? There's a reason it's called working out. Whether you're at the beach, in your backyard, or in a hotel room on the road, here are some moves that you can do anywhere, anytime.

1. WALKING FORWARD LUNGE WITH HIGH STEP

The great thing about lunges is that you can do them in endless variations, combining different stances with different kinds of terrain: sand, uneven ground, uphill. When you're lunging—wherever or however you do it—it's important to keep everything 90-degrees square. Your back is straight, your shoulders are pulled back (no hunching or leaning forward), your head faces forward, your hips are square. Your front knee aligns directly over your ankle; letting it jut over your foot will cause pain around the kneecap.

Begin this exercise by taking a wide step out front with your right leg, bending your right knee at a 90-degree angle above your right ankle (so that your shin is perpendicular to your thigh). Your left knee bends to touch the ground (right). Next, press off of your bent right leg and straighten it, simultaneously lifting your left leg forward and up, as if to take a giant step forward. Your left knee lifts to your chest; your right leg is strong and grounded (and your back continues to be straight). Step down onto your left foot, bending your left leg forward into a lunge. On your next step, lift your right leg forward and up with a high knee to complete the cycle. It's an exaggerated walking and lunging movement. Keep moving forward, alternating legs.

Try it: as an interval. Do 1 minute on; take 10 seconds off. Repeat 5 times.

Make it harder: Do the exercise in sand or going uphill.

2. WALKING LATERAL LUNGE

Instead of moving directly forward, lunge to a 45-degree angle on each leg. For these lateral lunges, skip the high step in between.

Try it: as an interval. Do 1 minute on; take 10 seconds off. Repeat 5 times.

Make it harder: Do the exercise going uphill.

3. HINDU SQUAT

In a Hindu squat, you complete the full range of motion. Ultimately, you want to be able to put your butt on your heels. (If you have to lift your heels off the ground to go lower, that's fine.)

Begin by standing with your arms at your sides, facing straight ahead. Your feet should be about 6 inches apart. Bend your knees and lower into a squat. At the same time, raise your arms forward so they're parallel to the ground (right). Press back up to standing, using your arms to help with the momentum and ending in the same position in which you started. Make sure to breathe on every repetition.

Try it: Do 40 reps nonstop in a slow, fluid motion.

Make it harder: Do 3 sets of 40 reps, with 20 seconds of rest in between. Gradually work your way up to 3 sets of 100.

4. DECLINE PUSHUP

Find a way to elevate your legs 1 to 2 feet off the ground. You can use a rock, a piece of furniture, a stump, a hillside—whatever's available. Working out in your environment is all about improvising and taking advantage of the surroundings.

Assume the pushup position, keeping your back straight and your core firm, making sure that your shoulders don't round forward. Your hands are aligned beneath your shoulders.

Try it: Do 30 pushups in this position.

Make it harder: Do as many pushups as you can complete in 2 minutes.

5. CORE SERIES

My friend Flavio De Oliviera showed me this sequence of 9 core movements. They're done in a progression, with no rest in between. You can adapt this routine in any way you'd like.

To begin: Lie on your back, using your hands to support your lower back. Lift your head slightly off the ground and look toward your toes. Keeping your stomach firm and your legs straight, raise your feet 6 to 12 inches off the ground. The closer your feet are to the ground, the harder these movements will be.

Movement #1: Lift your legs in a vertical scissoring motion. Keeping your legs straight, alternate raising your legs about 3 feet apart. Keep the motion fluid; when one leg comes down, the other goes up. Repeat 10 times on each leg (like an exaggerated flutter kick with straight legs).

Movement #2: Next, open your legs wide in a lateral scissoring motion. Keep your feet flexed and as close to the ground as possible. Make sure that your lower back doesn't arch (pressing your stomach muscles toward the ground also helps to stabilize your lower back). Do this 10 times.

Movement #3: Lift your legs straight overhead. Using your lower abdominals, press the soles of your feet skyward. Your hips should lift off the ground about 4 to 6 inches with each movement. Do this 10 times.

Movement #4: Slowly lower your legs to the ground. Bend your knees and bring them toward your chest. Do 10 crunches. Cradle your head in your hands, taking care not to pull on your neck with your hands and keeping your elbows out to the sides so they're aligned with your ears.

Movement #5: Extend your legs so that they're hovering just above the ground. Hold for 30 seconds. **Make it harder:** Pulse your feet up and down 2 to 3 inches while you're holding. Make sure that you're not holding your breath. Ideally, you will use your breath to work through these movements, inhaling and exhaling on each repetition.

Movement #6: Slowly lift your legs straight overhead again, feet flexed. Reach up with your right hand and touch your left foot. Alternate with your left hand touching your right foot. This movement combines reaching and twisting. Do this 10 times on each side.

Movement #7: Keeping your legs raised, reach your left arm down as far as you can, bending your left side as you do so. This will engage your left obliques (the muscles that enable bending and twisting) in a lateral crunch. Alternate from side to side. Do this 10 times on each side.

Movement #8: Place the soles of your feet together and let your knees fall out to the sides. Pressing your palms together, reach your hands toward your feet, and hold the contraction for a second or two before lowering slightly. This isn't a big movement—you don't want to lift your lower back off the ground. The point is to keep your core in a tight contraction for the entire set. Do this 10 times.

Movement #9: Lie flat on your back with your hands clasped behind your head. Lift your left knee to your chest, simultaneously raising your right foot 2 to 3 inches off the ground. Twist your right elbow to touch your left knee. Alternate sides by extending your left leg while bending your right knee toward your chest and twisting your left elbow to touch your right knee. This is a twisting, bicycling motion. Do this 10 times on each side.

Make it harder: Double the reps so that you're doing 20 of each movement.

6. HANDSTAND

I like to walk on my hands, but if you're uncomfortable with that, you can also do a handstand against a wall. Begin by facing the wall, kneeling. Place your hands flat on the ground about 3 inches from the wall, shoulder-width apart. Then straighten your arms and legs, and walk your feet toward your hands until your hips are approaching alignment above your shoulders. Keeping your arms straight and muscles firm, your shoulder blades pulled back and down, kick up with one leg to raise both legs above your head. Keep your head in a neutral position, looking down at your hands. Press through the soles of your feet, tighten your midsection, and press upward from your palms. This exercise builds back, shoulder, arm, and hand strength, and the inversion is good for circulation.

Try it: Hold for as long as you can, building to 2 minutes.

Make it harder: Do vertical pushups in this position, bending your arms and lowering your head toward the ground. Make sure you're very comfortable in a handstand before trying this.

7. DIPS

Find something that's 1 to 2 feet off the ground—in this case, I'm using a rock. A chair would also work; so would a bench or a ledge of some kind. Place your hands behind you with your palms flat and your fingers facing forward. Stretch your legs in front of you so that only your heels are touching the ground.
Next, bend your arms to a 90-degree angle, lowering your hips. Press to straighten your arms back up again.

Try it: Do 30 reps.

Make it harder: Do 3 sets of 30 reps.

8. THE STEEPS

Find a steep incline. A hill or a dune is ideal, but a long set of stairs will also work. The idea here is to get your heart pumping, to flush out some of the lactic acid you've generated with the anaerobic exercises that you've just done. I like to put on football cleats and do yard work on the hills around my house—it's great for flexing your ankles and really working them. The most important thing to remember when you're headed uphill is to use your whole foot, your ankles, and the backs of your calves. A lot of the time when people start climbing something steep, they move forward onto their toes. Don't do that. Flex your ankles and dig in.

Try it: For 15 minutes, walk briskly up and down your incline.

Make it harder: Move faster, bending your upper body forward to make your glutes and lower back work harder.

THE POWER OF YOGA

Growing up on Oahu's North Shore, I watched Gerry Lopez and Dick Brewer do yoga, so I was exposed to it early. It's an integral part of my fitness routine. I get peace of mind from yoga; it calms the brain. But it's also a great workout. If you think yoga's wimpy, you obviously haven't done it much. Think of the pose names: Warrior I. Warrior II. Genghis Khan's warriors did 1,000 sun salutations. That's serious.

DROPPING IN

NADIA TORAMAN

On the parallels between yoga and surfing and why no one should be afraid of a little bit of nirvana

❂ It's always great to teach yoga to athletes—it's one of my favorite things to do. And Laird is good at it; he's good at yoga in every way. One thing I appreciate about him is that if he's into it, he's really into it. In yoga, that helps because you have to be fully there. A lot of surfers like yoga—I think it's because when you surf, you're present; you're with the wave. You

I met Nadia Toraman about 15 years ago when she dropped in on a wave I was surfing. We had mutual friends, and I started going to her yoga class, which combines principles from Iyengar, ashtanga, and vinyasa. Nadia's an amazing teacher. Yoga is clearly her calling. In the pages that follow, she describes a series of postures that will help you build strength and flexibility (and don't be surprised if you also get a giant endorphin high).

actually become one with the wave. Yoga brings about the same state of mind. It awakens your awareness of the present moment. You're not doing the poses and thinking, *What's going on over there?* or *What is she wearing?*

✠ For a while Laird was doing two or even three classes a day. And it improved him, that kind of intensity. I think everyone should do that once in their lives; just dedicate themselves to the practice of yoga, whether it's for a week or, preferably, a month. All of us should indulge ourselves in that place; really take that time for body, mind, and spirit because otherwise the demands in our lives never let us get there.

✠ One reason I got into yoga was that I could not be still. My mind was all over the place. And now my favorite thing is to be still! For people who aren't doing yoga but want to start, my advice is not to be afraid of it, even if you feel like you're stiff. Just try it with an open mind. I think you'll find that yoga changes everything. It might only take one class to transform you. Literally, that single class—it's like watering a plant that has been dry. Even a couple drops of water make a difference to that plant. Exactly like that. And if you do it longer, just imagine how much more you will blossom.

YOGA

For all yoga practice, instructor Nadia Toraman recommends that you keep these foundations in mind.

BREATHING

In yoga, breathing is everything. The breath should be soft, smooth, and even, allowing the mind to be that way, too. Keep your inhalations and exhalations the same length, breathing mostly through the nose. When you breathe consciously (which we rarely do in life), you relax, and when you relax, you can stretch more fully.

ALIGNMENT

To properly hold a yoga posture, the body position is very precise. Think of the foundation of a building. If the ground floor is even a little bit off, then the walls will be off—everything will be off. You want to place your weight evenly on the four corners of both feet: mound of the big toe, mound of the small toe, and inner and outer heel. The feet are very important. From there, your leg muscles are firm. All four sides of your legs lift up. (A rule of thumb in yoga is that everything lifts up; nothing slumps down.)

Keep your pelvis in a neutral position. People tend to stand with their tailbones tucked too far under (in a slouch) or too far back (with an overly curved lower back). Imagine that you have a completely full bowl of water sitting at your hips and if you tilt in any direction, the water will spill. Your shoulders, hips, and heels are aligned. Your torso and shoulders are lifted (but make sure that your shoulders aren't hunched). Your chest should be wide open, your sternum lifted, your collarbones broad. Look straight ahead with your face and neck relaxed and your chin level. At the same time, your feet are grounded deeply into the earth. The rest of you goes up, toward the universe, the sky, the heavens.

SURYA NAMASKAR
Sun Salutation

Sun salutations are a series of movements that get the blood going and the body warmed up for the postures that follow. On their own, these moves are a good workout—you might want to do 5 to 10 of them in the morning to get the day started. If I want the class to sweat, I'll begin with a lot of these. If you want to move through the sun salutations more as a flow, hold each posture for 1 or 2 breaths. If you want to emphasize each posture, you can hold it for 10 breaths (or even 15 to 20 if you want to make it harder).

To begin, stand with your arms at your sides, your head relaxed and looking straight ahead, chin level. Feel the ground with your feet, and make sure that your weight is distributed evenly so your foundation is perfectly solid. Bring your hands to your heart in a prayer posture, and take 2 long smooth breaths. Then inhale and bring your arms overhead (right) as though you're reaching for the sun. Bring your palms together.

UTTANASANA
Standing Forward Fold

Next, fold your trunk over your legs. Your legs should be about 12 inches apart with your weight distributed evenly on both feet. Draw the top of your head down, keeping your shins, knees, and thighs in vertical alignment. Push your hips forward. As you bend, imagine drawing your thigh muscles upward while your shoulder blades move down your back toward your waist. Your torso, head, and neck should be relaxed. If you can't get your hands to the ground, you can place them on your shins or ankles. This is a calming position, excellent for curing a headache.

    Now look up, inhale, and, on the exhale, fold back into a forward bend (Uttanasana).

PLANK POSE

Inhale and step your feet back to plank position. Your hands are directly below your shoulders; your head is aligned with your spine. Lift one leg (below) for an optional variation. (If you do this, make sure you do it on both sides.)

CHATURANGA DANDASANA
Four-Limbed Staff Pose

In this pose, your body is held parallel to the ground by the strength of your legs and arms. Press the heels of your hands down, and pull your shoulder blades in toward your rib cage to keep your chest open and your back from hunching. Your elbows are tucked in toward your body. Keep your legs straight, and stretch them back slightly by pushing through your heels. Your body is an unbroken line. This is a strength-building pose, so if you want to challenge yourself, hold it as long as you can.

URDHVA MUKHA SVANASANA

Upward-Facing Dog Pose

From Chaturanga, lower your body to the ground. Press up through your palms into Upward Dog. In this pose, you really want to open your chest. To do that, slide your shoulder blades back and down, and press your heart forward. Your hands and the tops of your feet are planted, but your legs and hips are slightly raised off the ground. Take your head back without straining your neck or throat. Look upward to intensify the stretch.

ADHO MUKHA SVANASANA

Downward-Facing Dog Pose

Press the heels of your hands down, stretching your fingers and keeping your middle finger pointing directly forward. Also press down through the balls of your feet, stretching your heels back (and touching the ground with your heels if you can). Your head is aligned with your upper arms. Press forward with your chest, sliding your shoulder blades back. Keep your head and neck relaxed.

Now come back to standing. That's the cycle for one Sun Salutation.

UTKATASANA
Chair Pose

This is another strength pose, this time for your legs. With your feet together, squat down as though to sit. Lift your rib cage and stretch from your armpits as you reach your arms in the opposite direction of your hips. Basically, your body forms a dynamic zigzag. Keep your elbows straight, and look directly ahead.

Hold for 10 to 20 breaths.

UTTHITA TRIKONASANA
Extended Triangle Pose

Take a wide stance with your right foot facing forward and your left foot turned perpendicular to it. Lean over your right leg, placing your right hand on your ankle (or, if you're flexible enough, on the ground next to your right foot). Keeping your body on one plane—do not fall forward or backward with your upper body—stretch your left hand skyward. Look up at the thumb of your outstretched hand. Keep your shoulder blades pulled back and your chest wide open.

Hold for 5 to 10 breaths, and then switch sides.

UTTHITA PARSVAKONASANA
Extended Side Angle Pose

Take a wide stance with your right foot facing forward and your left foot turned perpendicular to it. With an exhalation, lower your right leg to a right angle and bend your torso over it. Place your right arm on your right leg (as shown) or on the ground next to your right foot. Stretch your left arm overhead with your palm facing down and your upper arm over your left ear. Feel the extension in one long line from your left ankle to the fingertips of your left hand. Turn your head and look up, making sure to keep your neck and face relaxed.

Hold for 10 to 15 breaths, and then switch sides.

VIRABHADRASANA I
Warrior Pose I

Stand straight with your arms at your sides. Step your right leg forward and bend it to 90 degrees, making sure that your knee and ankle remain aligned (your knee should not jut out in front of your ankle). Your right foot faces forward; your left foot is turned perpendicular to it. Your left leg is straight. Face forward with an open chest and your shoulder blades pulled back toward your rib cage. Stretch your back and arms upward, extending your spine from your tailbone. Both armpits are parallel to each other. Look toward your middle fingers, keeping your head and neck relaxed.

Hold for 10 to 15 breaths, and then switch sides.

VIRABHADRASANA II
Warrior Pose II

Stand straight with your arms at your sides. Step your right leg forward and bend it to 90 degrees, again making sure that your knee sits directly above your ankle. Your right foot faces forward, and your left foot is turned perpendicular to it. Your left leg is straight.

Extend your arms away from your torso at shoulder height, making sure that both arms are level. Keeping your back straight, stretch from your sternum through the tips of your fingers on both arms. Turn your head and look over your right fingertips.

Hold for 10 to 15 breaths, and then switch sides.

VIRABHADRASANA III
Warrior Pose III

This is the third and most difficult Warrior Pose. Begin by standing straight with your arms at your sides. Exhale and step forward with your left foot, simultaneously raising your right leg. Keep your left foot firm and your left leg strong and rooted. Reach forward, bringing your body weight onto your left leg and raising your right leg to hip level. Balance on your left leg, extending your right leg back, with your knee pointing down and your foot flexed. Stretch your arms and torso forward and parallel to the ground. Keep your head neutral or facing slightly forward.

Hold for 10 to 15 breaths, and then switch sides.

VASISTHASANA

Side Plank Pose

Start in Plank Pose (see page 80), and
then rotate your feet and torso 90
degrees to the left, keeping your feet
together. Stack your left side over your
right, keeping your head in line with your
sternum. Stretch your left arm overhead,
making sure not to let your hips sink. Look
up at your left hand, balancing on the
sides of your feet.

Hold for 10 to 15 breaths, and then
switch sides.

BAKASANA

Crane Pose

Stand facing straight ahead. Squat down
and place your hands flat on the ground
in front of your feet. Bend your knees and
elbows to your sides, resting the tops of
your knees on the backs of your upper
arms. Roll forward onto your palms,
keeping your head and chest forward.
Raise your feet, pressing your big toes
together and pointing them backward.
Straighten your arms and raise your torso
and legs as high as possible.

Hold for 5 to 10 breaths.

HANUMANASANA
Monkey Pose (Splits)

For full Hanumanasana: Stand facing straight ahead. Take a very wide step forward with your right leg so that you can place your hands flat on the ground, preferably right by your sides (as opposed to reaching forward). Work your heels apart, keeping your back erect and moving the base of your pelvis closer and closer to the ground.

For the version Laird is doing: Begin by kneeling, and then extend your right leg with your hands flat on the ground by your sides. Keeping your weight as evenly distributed above your hips as possible (try not to lean onto your right side), work your right leg forward with your left leg bent behind you. Face directly forward.

Hold for 10 to 15 breaths, and then switch sides.

SIRSASANA
Headstand

If you've never done this before, it's a good idea to practice against a wall. It's also advisable to have a yoga instructor demonstrate the fine points. You want your technique to be perfect so that nothing happens to injure your neck. Inversion poses are advanced, but once you learn them, they deliver enormous benefits, as they increase the flow of blood to the brain.

For Headstand, begin by kneeling with your hands clasped in front of you, the outer edges of your hands pressing into the ground. Place the crown of your head on the ground so that your clasped hands cradle the top of your head. Keep your elbows symmetrical so your head sits directly between them. Lean forward onto the top of your head, rolling your body weight onto your head and your clasped hands. Walk your feet toward your head, raising your hips until they approach alignment with your shoulders. Then you can either bend your legs to raise them above your head or, if you're strong enough, raise them in a pike position. Stretch upward from the soles of your feet.

Hold for as long as 20 minutes. If you feel any strain on your neck, stop immediately.

HALASANA
Plow Pose

Begin by lying flat on your back with your arms at your sides and palms to the ground. Inhale and bend your knees toward your chest. On the exhale, place your hands at the base of your lower back and straighten your legs. Slowly lower your legs to the floor behind you, keeping them straight. Breathe deeply, and on the exhale, work your legs backward to deepen the posture. If you feel any strain on your head or neck, stop. To come out of the pose, lift your legs above your head, bend your knees, and lower your legs to the ground. This is a great posture for stretching your back.

Hold for 10 to 15 breaths or longer.

SUKHASANA
Easy Pose

Begin by sitting with your legs outstretched. Fold your legs in toward your body, crossing them and placing each foot beneath the opposite knee so that the outer edges of your feet rest easily on the ground. Make sure that the base of your pelvis—your sit bones—is on the ground and you're not leaning forward. Make sure that your spine is erect and your back is not rounded. Pull your shoulder blades back and down, and open your chest so that your heart faces directly forward. Feel energy through the crown of your head while relaxing your head, face, and neck. Place your hands on your knees, palms facing up to receive whatever the universe offers.

You can hold this pose for as long as you'd like, taking long, deep breaths.

THERE'S NO SUCH THING AS NOT ENOUGH TIME

People think if they're working 14 hours a day that they're getting more done. Wrong. If you work for 11 hours and then do something physical for 3 hours, you'll be far more productive in those 11 hours than you'd be in 14. It takes energy to make energy. Otherwise you're just sitting at your desk in a daze, feeling overwhelmed by all the things you think you need to do. And then that goes on for years and it comes time to retire, but you're so out of shape you *still* can't do anything fun. That's messed up.

So when I hear someone say they don't have time for fitness—I'm not buying it. That's a cop-out. How can you *not* have time for your health and sanity? If you can't do a 2-hour workout every day, fine. But what about 30 minutes? Or 3 hours once a week to do something physically and mentally challenging, like hiking, biking, or kayaking? It's all about priorities. If you want to function at the highest possible level, you've got to move. Here's how you can do a lot for your body in a small amount of time.

USE YOUR ENVIRONMENT If you're in an office, take 10 minutes and run the stairs. And anywhere there's a wall, you can do wall squats, an energizing exercise that'll have your legs burning in 5 minutes. Just stand with your back flat against the wall, and lower your body until your legs are bent at a 90-degree angle, as though you were sitting with perfect posture but—sorry—no chair. Now hold that as long as you can. Rest for 15 seconds, and then do it again. Repeat as many times as possible.

USE YOUR BREATH To raise the degree of difficulty on anything—walking down the street, running for the bus, carrying groceries—hold your breath while you're doing it. Your heart rate will soar.

✥ **USE EVERY MINUTE** It's not about how long a workout takes; it's about how hard you make it. Over any given distance, you can jog—or you can sprint. If you have only 30 minutes at the gym, commit to going hard for every one of those minutes. Plan what you're going to do before you begin, and then dial up your intensity and keep it on high. And no water breaks. Sip from a bottle if you need to, but do it quickly as you move between exercises.

✥ **USE YOUR WHOLE BODY** In the Circuit (see page 47), we cycle through 15 exercises six times, adding extra abdominal moves in between. That takes from $2\frac{1}{2}$ to 3 hours to complete. But one of the beautiful things about circuit training is that once you understand its basic principles, you can create endless custom variations. You can vary the exercises, the number of reps, and the number of times you cycle through the set. You can design a circuit in which you change the order of the exercises on each round, or you can reverse the order on alternate cycles by doing it front to back and then back to front. There's no end to it. Plus, every gym contains different equipment, so you'll want to adapt your exercises to each new location.

Circuit training is perfect for short workouts. Here are some strategies for a great 30-minute whole-body workout.

Choose five exercises that, done together, work all your major muscle groups. For example:

✖ Squats		✖ Lunges
✖ Bent-over rows		✖ Bench presses
✖ Pull-ups	Or:	✖ Clean-and-jerks
✖ Chest flies		✖ Biceps curls
✖ Shoulder presses		✖ Seated rows

Arrange the order so you're alternating upper-body exercises with lower-body exercises.

In that order, do 20 reps of each exercise, moving quickly between them with no rest. Use a weight that makes it possible but difficult for you to complete all 20 reps.

Repeat this circuit three times. If your intensity is 90 percent or higher, and your heart rate reflects it, take a 1-minute rest interval between rounds. Otherwise, skip the rest and do the three rounds continuously. The goal is to wring as much effort as possible out of yourself in 30 minutes.

End the workout with a 5-minute superset of three abdominal exercises.*

- Alternating-leg bicycle twists (40 on each side)
- Side plank (hold for 1 minute on each side)
- Front plank (hold for 1 minute; rest 20 seconds; hold for 1 minute)

USE YOUR VACATION Vacations are an opportunity to upgrade your routine. You're out from behind the desk, and you've got time for yourself. I just took a heli-snowboarding trip to Alaska that was the perfect chance to work on my legs. I'd ride all day and then go for hikes through the deep snow before dinner. Try adding more activity than usual into your holidays. Once you sample a more active lifestyle—and see how it affects your mood, energy levels, and even your libido—I'd be surprised if you regressed to your prevacation routine.

---

*You can select any three abdominal exercises you'd like, but make sure to include at least one that targets your obliques.

RECOVERING

Injuries are a part of life. At least they've certainly been a part of mine. No one enjoys them, but if you avoided everything that might hurt you, you'd never get out of bed. What you need to do after an injury depends on the injury. Often it's best to work through it, but obviously for a big trauma that's not the case—you've got to do whatever is necessary to heal. Coping with pain, wounds, or other physical setbacks also requires mental strength. Keeping a positive attitude is critical. You never want to be less than 100 percent. And you won't be. State-of-the-art knowledge about injuries is fast advancing; there's an arsenal of things you can do, not just to heal well, but to do it quickly and without any negative long-term effects.

MY INJURY MAP

A TOUR OF MY WOUNDS: ALL THINGS CONSIDERED, IT'S NOT TOO BAD.

Broken eardrum
Again, at Pipeline. I was windsurfing in Kona winds. When you smack the water a certain way, your eardrum ruptures.

Lots of cuts. I'm the Cut King.

Boxer's fractures
I've broken my little fingers on both hands multiple times.

Ninety percent of my surfing injuries are on my left side because I'm a regular foot, meaning I lead with my left foot.

Broken and misplaced ribs
I've broken ribs numerous times. And I once blew a rib off my spine cliff jumping.

I've had a ton of stitches. At about 1,000, I stopped counting.

Surfboard to the femur
I got this cross-shaped scar on Christmas Day. This girl's surfboard speared my quad right down to the femur and bruised the bone. It took 3 months to heal. Basically, it was like someone took a pickax to my thigh.

Numerous punctures from surfboards.
There are some good ones on the insides of my thighs.

134 stitches in forehead
I was speared in the head by a surfboard at Pipeline when I was 14—134 stitches in my frontal lobe.

Surfboard through the cheek
I got a surfboard through my face in February 2007. The inside of my mouth was all exploded. It was like a 14-foot, 60-pound spear gun right behind my teeth, through the gums. If it had hit me in the temple, it would've been game over; see you in the next life.

First-degree shoulder separation
I separated my shoulder windsurfing at Hookipa. I did a flyaway kickout of a wave and landed on my board.

Chipped elbows
I've chipped both elbows falling and landing on things.

Herniated disk; crushed vertebrae
A Jet Ski landed on my back. I was surfing outside Hanalei Bay in Kauai with Nelly towing, and he got caught in the lip of a wave. I looked up and saw him coming, so I bent over, but it was basically a pile drive. It just plunged me into the water. There was a big dent in my back.

Skilsaw through the thigh
This happened in Kauai. I was cutting a board and as I finished, a piece of wood fell and hit my arm, which made the saw hit my leg. It cut through the top of my thigh, but it missed the fascia. The muscle was still intact, but it took 66 stitches to close it. I drove myself to the hospital.

Torn and reconstructed anterior cruciate ligament (ACL)
I blew out this knee twice. The first time was at Teahupoo. It was a freak accident. I flew out of a wave, and there was a boat right in front of me. I landed sideways, and my knee buckled. Then I blew it out again at Pe'ahi. I didn't have to have the operation, but I wanted it to be as strong as it could possibly be. This was the first surgery I've had and the first metal I've had in my body—a couple of tiny titanium screws. It's good. Doesn't give me any trouble.

Crushed top of foot
I dropped a 100-pound bench on my foot last fall. It broke a toe and dislocated the rest. I couldn't walk for 3 days. I think I'm going to need a pin or something in there.

Broken toes
I've broken every toe numerous times, except for my big toes. Many of my toenails haven't grown back. I've also sliced a toe in half.

Broken arches
My feet are just hammered. I've broken the arches a bunch of times. I'm not sure how many.

Broken ankle six times
My left ankle is my Achilles' heel. But amazingly, it still works just fine.

9 5

THE ANATOMY OF TROUBLE

STRATEGIES FOR DEALING WITH YOUR WEAKEST LINK

My left ankle is my Achilles' heel: I've broken it six times. The first time was when I was 16. I was out surfing in Kauai and got run over by a guy on a huge longboard. He had the early morning sun in his face, and he couldn't see. Ran straight into me. The impact broke my ankle, but then things got worse. I had to walk across this reef to get to shore, which caused the bone to break through my skin.

Since then I've snapped my ankle so many times that I've had some fairly dark moments wondering if I'd be able to surf again. There's nothing like a potentially career-ending injury to make you think. I recall times when I did things like cut casts off because they felt uncomfortable or played tennis on a broken leg. I haven't always been 100 percent smart about healing, but over the years I've come to learn what works and what doesn't. I've had a fair number of injuries where I've had to sit and watch giant swells go by—when you're hurt and you can't use your body, you quickly stop taking it for granted. These days, my left ankle works just fine, and I think that's due to a combination of luck and these strategies.

EARLY MOBILITY AND CONSTANT MOVEMENT The first thing I do for any kind of foot or ankle injury is head directly for the sand. Walking in loose sand is the ideal way to slowly strengthen the muscles and help recover a sense of proprioception, or feel for movement. The important thing is to do it barefoot, with the sand as your only support. That way your body works to stabilize your movements. If sand isn't available, most gyms have balance boards (or slabs of foam) you can stand on that will deliver the same sensation as sand. Anything that allows you to rock in any direction works for rebuilding ankle strength. In general, when rehabbing injuries, my theory is to be aware of your weakness, but don't coddle it.

✥ **ICING** Ice is a miracle cure, although it took me a while to learn that. Swelling is inflammation, which means the body's in a defensive mode rather than a healing one. Gabby and I both use a cold therapy system called Game Ready, which uses NASA spacesuit technology to deliver pressurized icing to the wound. It's high-tech and supereffective, but when it comes to icing, you can go as low-tech as a bag of frozen peas and still do your body some good.

✥ **NATURAL TREATMENTS** I use comfrey and arnica, both of which you can find at any good health food store. Comfrey is an herb that promotes healing of cuts, burns, bruises, and broken bones; its name comes from the Latin word *conferta*, meaning "grow together." Comfrey contains a naturally analgesic compound called an alkaloid (codeine is also an alkaloid). Use comfrey as a compress or a salve—don't ingest it. Arnica is a plant that's been used for medicinal purposes—to reduce muscle aches, bruising, and inflammation—since the 1500s. It's applied as an ointment or taken internally as a homeopathic remedy.

Another amazing natural product is Wobenzym. It's a proprietary mix of enzymes, created by a pair of German scientists in the '60s. It's also the most popular pain medication in Europe, used extensively for arthritis, joint pain, and injuries. Enzymes are critical for every chemical reaction in our bodies, and though internally we produce our own supply, the body's efficiency at doing this diminishes with age. Wobenzym's ingredients work synergistically to help the body heal itself, breaking down harmful proteins that cause inflammation.

✥ **ACUPUNCTURE** Acupuncture is a traditional Chinese medicine technique of inserting tiny needles into the body's energy meridians. Western medicine is also beginning to incorporate its theories, which have their roots in neuroscience—the acupuncture points are places where you can stimulate nerves, muscles, and connective tissue to boost your body's natural healing activity. If you don't think acupuncture

(continued on page 100)

NEAL S. ELATTRACHE, MD

In the past, if you busted yourself up, you were told to rest, lay off of it, apply a little ice. Not anymore. The goal of the best doctors now is to get you up and moving the injured body part as quickly as possible. In 2006, I had my first operation, a reconstruction of the anterior cruciate ligament (ACL) in my knee. My surgeon was Dr. Neal ElAttrache, head of the Kerlan-Jobe Orthopaedic Clinic in Los Angeles. His client list includes athletes from the NBA, NFL, NHL, and Major League Baseball; Olympians; dancers—all kinds of people who put high-performance demands on their bodies. Here, in his words, is his advice on how to heal.

❖ *Make It a Priority* Everyone has demands on their time and obligations they have to attend to, but it's critical to dedicate yourself to recovery, at least for a brief period of time. If you're distracted, if you're not goal oriented, if your mental outlook is to fight the process or be intimidated by the pain—it sounds simple, but you won't do well. If you do the right things with regard to diet and exercise, you will do well. And a positive attitude helps immensely.

❊ **Get Moving** Good physiotherapy is critical. For every moment you spend immobile or inactive, it takes twice as long to get back to where you were. And a lot of bad things happen in the process. For me, getting the patient up and moving is paramount. Now, whenever you have structures that are difficult to heal—like tendons, ligaments, or bones—you have to balance out the need for mobilization with giving the tissue a chance to become strong enough to mend. One of the ways we're addressing this is by improving our surgical procedures so they'll better withstand the rigors of movement.

❊ **Lifestyle and Diet Play a Role**
For healing, bone mineral supply is very important. The proper minerals are calcium, phosphorus, and magnesium. Vitamin C is critical to bone health as well. In general, keep your diet high in protein, vitamins, and minerals.

And whatever you do, don't smoke. Smoking is a big problem. It affects vascular health, and it's devastating to tissue healing in the body. When you're mending bones and joints, you're counting on tiny blood vessels— microvascular circulation—to be able to transport every bit of oxygen they can to the injured area. It's not like you've got big pipes of blood bringing that oxygen in. When you smoke, that microvascular circulation is the first thing to go. That's why in smokers you see a higher incidence of disk-related back problems and more difficulty healing bones and tissues. If you don't smoke and you've kept yourself in good physical condition, your blood vessels will thank you.

❊ **Consider the Future of Healing**
The new frontier is to enhance the biologic process of healing. We're doing things like isolating the growth factors from blood, concentrating them, and delivering that to where it needs to be. You're going to see stem cell–related biological manipulation happening over the next several years. It will really speed up the healing of injured tissue. It's a very exciting time. Kids born today are going to see amazing things done with tissue healing, cancer . . . things that could significantly lengthen people's lives. Now how we deal with one another as human beings when it's possible to really lengthen someone's time on earth, that's going to be a whole different problem.

works, you probably haven't tried it. In my experience, it's powerful stuff. The key is to get a great practitioner—ask around for a recommendation.

✥ HYPERBARIC OXYGEN CHAMBER This therapy is becoming standard practice for athletic injuries—many sports medicine clinics have them on site and use them to speed the recovery process. Basically, you're lying in a pressurized cubicle, which delivers a much higher concentration of oxygen into your body and therefore into your bloodstream. When the red blood cells are saturated with oxygen, injuries heal at a much faster rate. After my ACL reconstruction, I went twice a week to a clinic in Santa Monica, which rents these chambers by the hour. If you look around your area, you'll likely be able to find one.

✥ OCEAN THERAPY I'm a big believer in the healing properties of the ocean and made a point of immersing my ankles every day when they were healing. If the ocean isn't nearby, pour some sea salt or Epsom salts into a bucket or bathtub and soak in it. The trace minerals and elements in the salt will be absorbed through your skin.

IN PRAISE OF REST

You don't get stronger during training. You get stronger after your body rebuilds itself from training. That's why going hard all the time is an unproductive approach—it dulls both your mental and physical edges. Resting after a hard workout and giving your body what it needs to recover are the smartest things you can do.

✥ **FEED YOUR MUSCLES** Within an hour after training, you've got to eat—otherwise your body starts eating itself. You've just depleted its stores of energy and fluids, so it needs refueling. The time to do this is right after finishing a workout, when your system's craving glycogen. If you can eat (or drink) something that contains carbohydrates, proteins, and a bit of fat, you'll bounce back from exertion far more quickly. On the other hand, if you spike a bunch of sugar into your bloodstream by, say, drinking a Coke, you'll get a burst of energy, followed by a crash.

✥ **DRINK UP** It's as easy to get dehydrated after exercise as it is during it. There are dozens of fancy postworkout electrolyte-balancing recovery drinks available, but I generally avoid them because most are packed with sugar. Unless you're competing in a stage of the Tour de France, you can stick with water.

✥ **TAKE ACTIVE REST** Active rest—or movement that helps recovery—sounds like an oxymoron, but it's a big part of intelligent training. The key is to alternate activities that use your body in different ways. For example, after a heavy weight workout, I'll head out on a mountain bike ride. Following anaerobic exercise with something more cardiovascular helps flush lactic acid while circulating oxygen and other nutrients. Another way to approach active rest is to do something on your off days that gets you moving but isn't a grind. Go for an easy swim. Kick back with a game of bocce on the beach. Not only will it give your muscles a break, it's a license to play that will help you stay motivated.

GET ENOUGH SLEEP (AND MAYBE A LITTLE EXTRA) Never skimp on sleep. When I'm working hard, exerting myself physically, I'm an 8- to 10-hour-a-night guy. Not that I can't operate with less, but over the long haul, I need at least 8 for a sense of well-being. That downtime is vital to your body's ability to regenerate itself. All kinds of critical processes take place while you're sleeping, including the pituitary gland's biggest pulse of growth hormone. Your brain's pumping out different wavelengths; your muscles get a chance to relax completely. Disrupting your natural sleep cycle is one of the most damaging things you can do. (And by the way, it's not true that you can catch up on missed sleep.) If you consistently get less sleep than you need over a prolonged period, it will negatively affect every system in your body. Don't feel guilty about being horizontal. On the contrary: If you need more rest, take it.

AND ENJOY IT Relax—you've earned some time off. Lie around. Nap. Get a massage. It took me a while to learn this, but now when I feel burnt out, I lift my legs up on the couch and enjoy it.

EATING

EAT FOR PERFORMANCE, HEALTH, AND (LET'S NOT FORGET) PLEASURE.

SIMPLE PHILOSOPHIES FOR HEALTHY EATING

❖ **WORK UP AN APPETITE** I don't like to eat unless I'm hungry. When I sit down to a meal, I want my body to be in a state of craving. I'll start the day with a protein shake (see page 139), something that's easy to digest so my body doesn't have to work so hard. But I won't have a full breakfast until later, after I've spent a few hours out on the water or working on my land. Not eating until you're hungry means that you're not snacking much, if at all. I realize that some people love it, but the idea of grazing throughout the day is not for me.

❖ **EAT CLOSE TO THE SOURCE** If I can't pronounce it or don't know what it is, it's not going into my body. In Hawaii, we're fortunate that we still have access to real food from the earth. Beware of any "food" that has been created by humans rather than nature.

Have you ever really looked at the labels on processed food? The list of ingredients is surreal. Here's one: perfluorooctanoic acid (PFOA). Sounds like something you'd find in battery acid, not food. But it's in microwave popcorn, added to make the bag less flammable. If PFOA sounds like a toxic chemical, that's because it is; in fact, it's been designated a likely carcinogen. And there are countless examples like this. Some chemicals are put into food to make the stuff last for months; some are added for cosmetic reasons—for coloring, flavoring, sweetening, texture, smell, you name it. Most of these additives haven't been around that long, and their long-term effects on humans are unknown. Which means that if you eat them, you're the guinea pig.

⟡ FOOD CRAVINGS ARE IMPORTANT We all need to listen to our bodies. If you suddenly have a craving for something like pecans or carrots, I think that's a real indication that your body's looking for something, some mineral or element found in a certain type of food. You have to figure out what the craving really means. If you're dying for chips, it could be that you need to eat something salty (but healthier), like edamame. Cravings have a bad reputation because they're often related to sweets. I'm not saying you should run out and indulge your desire for doughnuts or candy; if your body wants sugar, the best thing to eat is fruit.

⟡ DIVERSITY RULES I believe that it's important to eat a widely varied diet. If you're traveling, don't pass up an opportunity to try the local foods just because there's a burger joint down the street. In Alaska, for instance, I've eaten reindeer sausage (which is delicious, like all venison); in Indonesia, I'll always go for durian fruit (don't hold its moldy-sweat-socks-with-a-hint-of-sulfur smell against it; durian has an amazing custardy flavor). Another strategy to mix it up is when you grocery shop, don't just buy the same stuff every time. The food universe is vast, and in it there are countless nutrients, minerals, enzymes, bioflavonoids, phytochemicals—all kinds of elements. There are hundreds of essential fatty acids, whole classes of building blocks with names you've probably never heard of—things like eicosanoids, lipoxins, isofurans, and neuroprotectins. Each one of them provides your cells something unique. That's why the more diverse your diet, the healthier you're going to be. Add unusual spices, salts, seeds, condiments, seaweeds, fruits, and vegetables to your menu—there are countless things you can try. One thing I always appreciate is that when Gabby cooks, she never makes anything the same way twice. Every one of her meals has its own flair.

❖ DON'T EAT DEAD FOOD Pasteurization is the process of taking raw dairy products and cooking them at high temperatures to kill off bacteria so the food will have a longer shelf life. The problem with pasteurization is that it also destroys the food's *good* bacteria, along with much of its proteins and vitamins. And mainstream dairy products also get homogenized, which means they're forced through a fine screen that breaks their fat molecules down (so they don't separate into layers). This changes the food's entire molecular structure, but hey, it'll keep for 6 months! Homogenization and pasteurization turn dairy products into dead foods. That's why many people can't tolerate milk; our bodies reject these end products because they're so alien. I don't consume a lot of cheese, butter, or milk, but when I do, I go for unpasteurized or raw.

Another thing to watch out for is food irradiation (sometimes called electronic or cold pasteurization). And yes, that means exactly what it sounds like. Irradiated food has been nuked. Once again, nutrients are stripped away in favor of making the food last longer. No one has any idea what long-term health problems might be caused by eating food that's been blasted with radioactivity, but genetic mutation and cancer are suspected as possibilities. The Europeans have banned the process, but in America, the FDA has endorsed it for all kinds of foods, including lunchmeat in schools. *No thanks.*

❖ MAKE QUALITY A PRIORITY Yes, it's more expensive to buy organic food. It's also true that cooking high-quality meals from scratch takes time—it's not as convenient as buying prepared or packaged foods. But here's the thing: When you put something into your mouth, you might enjoy it for 5 seconds, but your system will be dealing with its repercussions for a long time. Often people eat what their tastebuds want and not what their bodies need. You know that Taco Bell isn't the best dietary choice, but you go there because it's easy and you like the taste. When you're young you might be able to do this and still have a lot of energy. In the end, though, it'll catch up with you. Potato chips in = potato chips out. That's the rule.

Spend money; get quality food. Get fresh fish and free-range, organic meat. In particular, make sure to upgrade anything you eat on a regular basis. If you're drinking coffee every day, drink the best coffee you can find. It always amazes me when people say that eating well is too expensive—but then they'll go out and buy a giant plasma TV. So you're eating like crap but you're staring at a nice screen. Not too smart.

✥ **IN ALL OF THIS, DON'T BE OBSESSIVE** I have friends who eat healthier than anyone, but it takes them 3 hours to prepare a meal. They measure their food out by the gram, and if they don't have their macrobiotic tofu, they go into a seizure. I don't want to be that temperamental. If I get into a position where I have to eat an airplane meal or a Big Mac, I'm not going to love it, but it won't put me into toxic shock. It's like if a car is too high performance, then it's sensitive to any impurities in the fuel. I'm more like a diesel truck. If a little water gets in there, it's still going to be okay.

✥ **AND REMEMBER TO ENJOY YOURSELF** People spend a lot of energy worrying about whether they're eating the right thing or how many calories something has. As a culture, we rush through our meals because we think we've got far more important things to do. All too often, we take our food for granted. I'm always reminding myself to eat more consciously; to chew slowly and savor what I'm eating. (You can't bolt down your dinner while watching *CSI* and then wonder why you have digestive problems.) Nature has given us millions of unique flavors; our job is to explore them and appreciate every one.

10 *FOODS* THAT I *LOVE* . . .

I love sushi, I love Japanese food, I love Hawaiian food—I love food in general.
But when I get down to specifics, these are the 10 things I'd have the hardest time
giving up.

1. ORGANIC, FREE-RANGE BEEF Meat's at the top of the list. I'd last about a week
(maybe) as a vegetarian. Everyone's biochemistry is different; some people thrive on a
high-carbohydrate diet. I'm not one of them. Free-range meat is among the most
nutritious of all foods and a huge source of vitamin B. Venison's also great; so is elk.
The closer to the wild, the better.

2. LOCALLY CAUGHT OPAH Opah, also known as moonfish, is a whitefish found in
Hawaiian waters. It lives at depths between 50 and 400 meters down, often in the
company of tuna and billfish. Opahs don't travel in schools, which means they aren't
easily overfished. They're great for sashimi, as well as broiling or grilling. You may or
may not be able to find opah where you live, but it's worth finding out whether there's a
local catch of some kind in your area. Frozen fish, while it may be convenient, is
nothing like fresh.

3. PAPAYA A perfectly ripe papaya is a beautiful thing. Along with its delicious
taste, it contains papain, an enzyme that helps digest proteins and acts as a
natural anti-inflammatory in your system. Papaya's also rich in antioxidants
(a special class of vitamins that help repair cell damage), including vitamin C
and folic acid.

4. PINEAPPLE Pineapple is another awesome fruit. Like papaya, it contains a powerful
digestive enzyme, this one called bromelain (which helps heal bruising). Pineapple's

loaded with antioxidants, too, as well as a trace mineral called manganese, which is essential to build bone and connective tissue. The riper the pineapple, the more nutrients it contains.

5. MUSTARD I love the old-fashioned stone-ground stuff. It's a flavor that really appeals to me, so this fact is a bonus: Mustard is so dense with minerals, phytonutrients, and omega-3 and omega-6 fatty acids that up until the 20th century, it was considered a medicine rather than a food.

6. RAW BUTTER Real, unprocessed butter is amazing. Before homogenization and pasteurization blunt its nutrients, butter contains nearly 500 essential fatty acids. When you heat real butter, it turns clear. When you heat homogenized butter, it turns black.

7. CASHEWS Cashews are my favorites (with macadamias as a close runner-up), but I like all nuts. They get a bad rap for being high in fat and calories, but the fats they contain are beneficial ones like oleic acid, which promotes cardiovascular health. And though they're not low calorie, those fats combined with the nuts' protein mean a handful of cashews or almonds will keep you going for a long time. Try that instead of an energy bar sometime, and you'll see what I mean.

8. POI In Kauai I grew up eating poi, a traditional food made from the taro plant. In Hawaiian culture, both taro and poi have spiritual significance. Growing the plant, harvesting it, and then roasting it and pounding it into a thick paste—all of this is a sacred ritual. Not everyone likes poi's subtle, unusual taste, and you're not likely to run into it on the mainland, but if you have a chance to try it, I recommend that you keep an open mind.

9. ALEA SEA SALT This salt is a combination of pure sea salt and alea, a medicinal red clay; both are mined in Hawaii. The clay gives the salt a beautiful red tint. I happen to like this one, but there are dozens of unique sea salts that you can add to your diet. Each one has a slightly different taste, color, and mix of trace elements. This is something that comes straight from the earth—the composition of minerals in unprocessed sea salt is so intricate that it can't be reproduced in a lab. Your typical table salt has been stripped of its trace minerals but does have additives, including aluminum. And besides that, compared to sea salt, it tastes awful.

10. POISSON CRU I discovered poisson cru, a kind of ceviche in coconut milk and lime juice, when I went to Tahiti in 2001 to surf the wave called Teahupoo. Since then I've been back several times, and I've put away my share of this local dish. If you like sashimi, this stuff is over the top (see the recipe on page 134).

... AND A *FEW* THAT I *DON'T*

My approach isn't total abstinence; that's a little excessive. But these are the foods I avoid on a regular basis.

1. BREAD Bad bread—that doughy, gummy kind you can mash up and turn into a Super Ball—is gnarly. You can throw a wad of that stuff into water and it doesn't even break apart.

Better-quality bread is slightly more tolerable, like a baguette fresh out of the oven if you're in France, but if I eat any bread, it makes me want to go to sleep. I don't go for sandwiches, either. They make me feel bloated and stuck.

In general, I avoid wheat and other starchy foods. I'm not big on potatoes, rice, or pasta, either. I'm not saying I'll never eat a waffle, but it's a rare thing, and I'm not going out of my way to do it.

2. PIZZA I know most people love it, but to me, you might as well wet down some cardboard and add ketchup. My teeth get a chalky feeling just thinking about it.

3. SODA Can't imagine drinking the stuff. Soda contains zero nutrients—no vitamins, no minerals, nothing beneficial. Plus, it makes you fat and acidifies your system (which is meant to be slightly alkaline), so to buffer that, your body leaches calcium from your bones and teeth. With all its refined sugar and chemicals, soda's about as far as you can get from a healthy, living food.

4. CHEESE Although on occasion I don't mind some nice Brie on a cracker, I'm not a big cheese guy. When I do eat it, I want it unpasteurized (see page 107). In the US, our selection of raw cheese is small. You go to Europe, that's when you get spoiled. In France they tried to get rid of raw cheese and almost had a civil war.

TUNA

In our house we love sashimi, especially tuna. Fortunately, it's easy to get fresh, locally caught ahi and yellowfin in Hawaii. But these days, all tuna comes with a health warning due to the high levels of mercury found in its flesh. Children and pregnant or breastfeeding women are most at risk, but no one wants to ingest a neurotoxin. Most mercury pollution comes from industrial sources like coal-fired power plants, which release it into the air. Then it settles into the environment, where it accumulates in the food chain. Tuna and other predators like sharks and swordfish are at the top of this chain and therefore consume other animals—and more mercury. Because of this, tuna isn't something you should eat every day. A good source for information about mercury in tuna is www.oceana.org.

As if that's not enough bad news, tuna also faces the problem of being unsustainably fished in many places. Bluefin populations are in dire straits worldwide. And while ahi and yellowfin are still rated among the best seafood choices, it's important to understand where your fish came from and how it was caught. For instance, yellowfin or ahi caught by trolling or with poles (as they are in Hawaii) is good, but you want to avoid fisheries (in other parts of the world) that catch them on a longline. Longlining produces bycatch, which means that other ocean creatures like seabirds, sea turtles, dolphins, and sharks get wastefully killed in the process. The Monterey Bay Aquarium produces up-to-date regional guidelines about which kinds of seafood are best in which regions and which should be avoided: www.montereybayaquarium.org.

MY MUST-TAKE SUPPLEMENTS LIST

Our ancestors got their critical nutrients from their diet. These days we don't have that option. Our topsoil's depleted, and our grocery stores are filled with food that's been processed, denatured, and tweaked. To optimize your nutrition, along with eating well, you need to add other sources. Here are the supplements that I rely on.*

✥ **NEURO 1** I take Neuro 1 powder every day. Basically, it's a brain supplement that works on your focus, short-term memory, and motivation. My friend Bill Romanowski, the former linebacker and four-time Super Bowl champ, developed it to help himself recover from numerous concussions. Working with doctors and scientists, he developed a cutting-edge mix of vitamins, minerals, and brain-support nutrients like phosphatidylserine (a fatlike molecule that's a key part of neuron membranes). Healthy neuron membranes are important: They're what's standing between you and dementia. And they're highly vulnerable to wear and tear, something that all of us begin to notice as we age. Suddenly it's no longer quite so easy to remember where we left the car keys.

✥ **CATIE'S ORGANIC GREENS** If perfect health came in powder form, it would look exactly like this stuff. Catie's is the real deal. One tablespoon equals seven servings of green vegetables in a form that your body can easily assimilate. Aside from delivering great nutrition, Catie's helps balance your body's pH levels. This is important because many diseases, including cancer, can only thrive in an acidic environment.

✥ **CATIE'S VITAMIN C PLUS** This is the sibling of Catie's Greens, but instead of vegetables, it mostly involves fruits. Along with what it does contain—a megadose of antioxidants (a class of vitamins that help heal cell damage)—I like this product for what it doesn't: the synthetic chemicals and sugar that are added to many vitamin C powders.

---

*Full disclosure: I have no financial interest in any of these products, and where there's any kind of relationship, I say so. With supplements, as with anything else, there's a sliding scale of quality. The bottom line is that, for me at least, these work.

COLLOIDAL SILVER Colloidal silver, a suspension of ultrafine silver particles in demineralized water, is a natural antibiotic and disinfectant. I use it to treat ear infections and for cleaning cuts—and unlike hydrogen peroxide, it kills bacteria, viruses, and fungi without harming enzymes or tissue. Some people take colloidal silver internally, but I only use it topically. Quality can vary; avoid brands that tell you to shake or refrigerate them. That means they contain additives or that the silver particles aren't dispersed properly.

FRESH NONI Noni is a fruit that the Polynesians use to remedy everything from migraine headaches to diabetes to cancer. It contains a potent medicinal alkaloid called proxeronine, which helps damaged cells mend themselves. It's also a blood purifier, an immune system booster, and a digestive stimulant, and it helps the body remove toxins. Unfortunately, noni smells like vomit and tastes absolutely vile. When you first take it, you break into a sweat instantly. If you can get past that, it's unbelievably good for you.

UDO'S OILS I think people underestimate the importance of high-quality fats and oils in their diet. These fats are the basis for all cell activity—every system in your body needs them to operate, and your only way of getting them is through diet. The body doesn't manufacture its own supply. I like Udo's Omega 3-6-9 Oil because it's made from the purest sources, and it contains the right ratios of omega-3 to omega-6.

MUSCLE MILK PROTEIN POWDER There's no shortage of protein powders to choose from, but I like this brand because it's easy to digest. After that it's my usual criterion: zero or minimal added sugar; the highest-quality ingredients balanced in the right ratios; easily absorbed by the body; no chemicals or fillers.

AWESOME FOODS YOU MIGHT NOT KNOW ABOUT

✥ **QUINOA** It's considered a grain but is actually related to leafy green vegetables like spinach and Swiss chard. Unlike other grains, it's a complete protein, which means it contains all nine essential amino acids. Quinoa (pronounced "KEE-no-ah") has a nice nutty flavor and an interesting texture that's both chewy and crunchy. It's also gluten free. The ancient Incas considered quinoa a sacred food; they called it chisaya mama, or "the mother of all grains."

✥ **KOMBUCHA** On paper, kombucha ("kom-BOO-cha") sounds nasty: a culture of yeast and bacteria that's mixed with black tea and sugar and then fermented. In reality, the end result is a tart (but great tasting), slightly effervescent, low-calorie, high-nutrient drink that energizes and detoxifies your body, balances your internal pH, and curbs your appetite. It's all natural with zero preservatives and comes in various brands and flavors. It's becoming wildly popular, so your local health food store is likely to carry it.

✥ **HEMP MILK** Yes, the hemp plant is related to marijuana. No, hemp is not illegal, and it won't get you high. Here's what hemp is: one kick-ass plant. It's been cultivated for more than 10,000 years and can be used for everything from fabric to biofuel to lotion to paper to food—and in this case, a superior alternative to milk. Hemp has the most potent source and the highest content of essential fatty acids (omega-3 and omega-6) of any plant, and it's rich in calcium, amino acids, B vitamins, and fiber. Hemp milk is a relatively new product, better tasting and better for you than soy milk, and it's not full of bovine growth hormone or pasteurized like cow's milk. You can find it at good natural foods stores, including Whole Foods.

✥ **AGAVE NECTAR** This comes from the agave plant, which is also the source for tequila. It's the natural sweetener with the lowest glycemic index, which means your body doesn't process it like a simple sugar. And yet it's 75 percent stronger than sugar—so sweet that you never need more than a tiny amount.

IN PRAISE OF THE WEIRD

I like to try strange fruits and vegetables, things like lychee nut or durian fruit. Variety is key; if you eat colorful, interesting foods, you'll expose yourself to new worlds of flavors. And if you think about it, that's what makes eating fun.

AÇAI Native to the Brazilian Amazon (but widely available in the US now), the purple açai (pronounced "ah-sigh-EE") palm fruit has 30 times the amount of antioxidants of red wine and also contains a large dose of essential fatty acids. In other words, these berries, which taste nutty with hints of chocolate, are nature's own vitamin pills. I like to mix up a bowl of açai, bananas, and granola for breakfast.

SEAWEED Any sea vegetable, I'm into. There are hundreds of edible seaweeds. My favorite is one the Hawaiians call limu kohu, and it's a delicacy. I also like nori and the seaweed salads you'll find at a good Japanese restaurant. They all contain minerals and elements you won't get anywhere else, straight from the source. Talk about your basic nutrition—sea vegetables are like primordial nutrition.

LILIKOI Lilikoi is a type of passion fruit that grows wild in Hawaii. It's an egg-shaped yellow fruit with a tough shell that contains a translucent pulp. This pulp and its seeds are the edible parts. A friend of ours strains lilikoi and makes juice, and people often add it to desserts as a flavoring, but my favorite way to eat it is right off the vine.

PAUL CHEK

To say that this man has strong ideas is an understatement. I met Paul Chek at his C.H.E.K. (Corrective Holistic Exercise Kinesiology) Institute in Encinitas, where he teaches athletes and trainers from every corner of the planet how to maximize their potential—rather than working against themselves, as we all do from time to time. Talking to Paul, you quickly realize that he's forgotten more about health and fitness than other experts knew in the first place. His philosophy blends body, mind, and soul in cutting-edge ways. In particular, his insights about food and eating have resonated with me. Here, he shares that wisdom.

✛ I was a boxer on the army boxing team, then I became the trainer. For 2 years I did all the sports massage, wrote all the nutritional programs and all the exercise programs for 30 of the best boxers in the world.

✛ I'm constantly amazed—perplexed, actually—at how all these people with master's degrees and PhDs in health and medicine can't even keep themselves healthy. They don't eat right, and they don't know how to take care of themselves. Some of the sickest people in the world are at nutrition conferences. Blows my mind.

- Every 6 months, the army athletes had to see a nutritionist—it was mandatory. And they hated it because the nutritionist was about 5'4" and weighed 230 pounds. She'd sit there and tell them their diets should be 70 percent carbohydrates and that eating sugar was fine. She endorsed low-fat and artificially sweetened products—and that was the opposite of what I was telling them. I told them to eat living foods.

- I do a very comprehensive analysis. It takes people about 4 hours just to fill out the paperwork. I look at you physically, emotionally, mentally, and spiritually, and I have an elaborate system of analyzing where you're stuck in your life: where you're not moving, where your problems are coming from, or where you're likely to get them. I can see energy building up in your body or in your emotional, mental, or spiritual energy fields. I can see it and I can feel it.

- The toughest people to treat are the ones who think they're healthy, but they're really unhealthy. Like nutritionists.

- Laird was what I call unconflicted. Energy moves through him efficiently. There's no blockage. Laird doesn't need somebody's approval to be Laird. I didn't have to do a lot with him. I only had to fine-tune. Like most athletes, he was just working too much.

- The "right diet" is different for everybody. You're the biological product of the mix of your genes. So if your father was an inland aboriginal, an ideal diet for him would have been about 90 percent carbohydrate and 10 percent animal food. But if your mother was an Eskimo, her ideal ratio was 90 percent fats and proteins and only 10 percent carbohydrates. So if an aboriginal marries an Eskimo, you've got two extreme opposites of diet—and their children can be anywhere in between.

- Fat is critical in your diet. We need it. But it has to be clean fat. If you eat commercially raised animals, it can be very poisonous because fat is where toxins accumulate. And they allow the feeding of things like manure, plastic chips, sawdust, antibiotics, and heavy steroids—the

(continued)

load is so heavy that the animal has to keep making more fat to store the toxins in. And then they sell the meat by the pound!

- Always go out of your way to purchase organic, free-range meat. It's far more nutritious, and it's pesticide, hormone, and antibiotic free. If that's not available, the next best choice is grass-fed meat. At least the animals were free to roam, getting exercise and eating what they were designed to eat.
- Every molecule of everything you eat affects your physiology, your endocrinology, and your psychology as long as it remains in your body.
- The fact is, if you eat anything that's less alive than you, to the degree that it's less alive than you, you have to spend your own life force to turn it into human tissue. The longer anything lasts on the shelf, the more dead it is. Remember, you're turning over two million blood cells per second. The question I ask people is: What'd you make them out of? Doughnuts? Coca-Cola? Kelloggs' Frosted Flakes? That's all garbage.
- The average American eats his body weight in food additives each year, or approximately 150 pounds. Always look at the label: If there are words you don't understand there, chances are good your body won't like whatever it is, either.
- When people eat incorrectly, they get tired. When they get tired, they drink coffee and eat more sugar. And that shuts the immune system down. One teaspoon of sugar shuts the immune system down for approximately 6 hours.
- On the weekend, don't take any supplements, so your body doesn't forget to absorb nutrients out of your food. You want the body to reach for them, not to get lazy.
- I drink no alcohol. I don't even like it. It makes me sick. But I teach my students the 80/20 rule: Live right 80 percent of the time; party 20 percent of the time. If you do what I teach you 80 percent of the time, you can stand a binge.

ED STEWART

In the small town of Paia on Maui's north shore, you'll find a coffee shop called Anthony's that's run by my friends Ed and Keri Stewart. When it comes to breakfast—and especially to shots of their hand-roasted Italian espresso—Anthony's is like my second home when I'm on the island. Here, Ed shares the backstory.

✤ Keri and I moved from the Seattle area. We came to Maui to look at a business on the other side of Lahaina. We wanted to open a coffee shop, but when we saw the space, next door to it was a Harley-Davidson store. I said, "Well, we're here. There's this cute little town, Paia. We might as well go have a look over there." So we did. And we walked by this building and saw some guy installing a coffee roaster. We came in and started talking to him. His name was Anthony Campbell. The place wasn't even open yet. We told him, "Well, here's our card; if you ever want to sell it, call us."

✤ When we got home, there was a message that Anthony had called. I called him back. "You want to buy my business?" he said. "I've been open 3 days. I hate the public."

✤ We did the deal on a handshake, and 3 weeks later we were running the place. Anthony taught us how to roast coffee. That was 12 years ago.

⁜ I didn't know who Laird was when he first came in. He loved coffee; he always wanted shots of espresso, which was different because the surfing community was usually lighter in their morning habits, like tea or cold drinks. And one day he asked Keri if she could make him a tuna melt. It was 7:00 a.m. And I'm thinking, *Who in the world is eating a tuna melt at this time of the day?* But Laird always knew his diet. The only healthy thing we had at that time was tuna. So I got this little toaster oven out, made him an open-faced tuna melt.

⁜ We became friends because he's just a very generous man. Laird is Hawaiian in his heart. He respects other people. When he's gone, everyone's bored! When he and Gabby and the kids come back in the fall, everybody's happy. He brings a party to the table.

⁜ Since the tuna-fish sandwiches years ago, we've put in a kitchen. So now Laird has a selection. We keep New York steaks on hand and fresh ahi.

⁜ One day his breakfast might be a New York steak with four poached eggs and a green salad with tomatoes and avocados. The next day it'll be an ahi steak. He's eating a dinner in the morning; his day has been going since the sun came up.

⁜ Our cook, Val Akana, grills the steak with Montreal Steak Seasoning. For the fish, it's just a little light seasoning on both sides. Laird is pretty straightforward in his eating habits—fish should taste like fish. He's not smothering things with hollandaise sauce or anything like that.

⁜ In Hawaii, we have avocados that are as big as footballs. They don't ship them to the rest of the US. There are various kinds, but the butter avocado is what we use. It's a lighter green outside, and when you slice it, it's just real smooth. It also has a very full-bodied flavor.

⁜ From top to bottom, we're making our own coffee. We even print the labels ourselves. This year we started Anthony's Estate coffee. We're growing the beans on a hillside in Kula. It's all organic and we handpick it, mill it, and roast it.

⁜ This shop has been really great for us. We didn't think we'd be doing it this long. At the end of the day I can't think of anything else I'd rather do—except maybe live Laird's life.

ON ESPRESSO VERSUS DRIP

I love everything about espresso—the smell, the taste, the ritual of grinding the beans. On an average day, I'll drink between four and eight shots over the course of the morning, either straight up or as an Americano (with more water). While some coffees give you a jittery feeling, espresso doesn't affect me like that. It revs up my body in a low-impact way; the energy I get from it is steadier. I attribute that difference to the way espresso is processed. It's the darkest of all roasts, which means they've burned out most of the impurities—the chemicals, fertilizer, pesticides, sulfites, anything absorbed by the plant where it's being grown. By contrast, I think the worst coffee is that clear-looking stuff you see sitting around on burners in restaurants. Those kinds of beans usually aren't dark roast, so they're slightly green to begin with; then, through the drip process, the coffee sits in water for a longer time, allowing impurities to leach into the liquid. With espresso, the water is heated, then quickly steamed through the beans. A shot of espresso has less caffeine than drip coffee while delivering more antioxidants. And though it has a stronger flavor than lighter coffees, espresso is less acidic, so it doesn't upset your stomach. The Europeans have it right. They're coffee connoisseurs and won't touch the drip stuff. You'll have a hard time finding a Bunn-o-Matic in Italy.

WATER

In many parts of America we have surprisingly good tap water, but people shy away from it. It's true that minerals are added to our water supply, but sometimes I wonder if it's better to drink chlorinated water out of the tap than it is to drink pure spring water out of plastic bottles. Sure, you're drinking something pristine—but it's in a plastic bottle. The list of chemicals used to make a plastic bottle is like something out of The Twilight Zone and includes some of the scariest substances out there. Phthalates and bisphenol A, two of the most common plasticizing chemicals (used to make the material soft, shatterproof, inflammable, etc.), are both known to cause reproductive and endocrine system problems.

Plastic bottles are also a massive environmental scourge, especially in the ocean. Ninety percent of floating marine debris is plastic, and once a wayward water or soda bottle gets in there, it becomes more than a blight on the scenery and a hazard to sea creatures; the bottle's mix of petroleum and toxic chemicals becomes part of the food chain. If you don't trust tap water, then consider putting a filtration system in your house. If you feel you must buy bottled water (or any other bottled drinks), go for glass containers.

MY GROCERY SHOPPING LIST

The list varies from week to week, but my philosophy is always the same: I buy organic, unprocessed, fresh food.

ANIMAL PRODUCTS

Eggs and Cheese

Fertile, free-range, and local eggs

Feta cheese

Unpasteurized (raw) Cheddar

Fish

Opah (or other fresh, local whitefish)

Tuna (yellowfin, ahi)

Wild Alaskan salmon

Meat and Poultry

Free-range, grass-fed New York steak

Lean ground beef

Free-range organic chicken

FRUITS

Bananas

Berries, fresh and frozen (all kinds)

Fresh-squeezed organic orange juice

Organic apple juice

Organic cherry juice

Papayas

Pineapples

VEGETABLES AND LEGUMES

Avocados

Beans (navy, pinto, lima, cannellini)

Beets

Broccoli

Brussels sprouts

Green beans

Kale

Lentils

Mustard greens

Poi

Purple potatoes

Quinoa

Spinach

Squash (spaghetti, zucchini, butternut)

Sweet potatoes

NUTS

Almonds

Cashews

Macadamia-nut granola bars

Pine nuts

GRAINS

Fresh corn tortillas

Rice (brown, wild)

Rolled oats

MISCELLANEOUS

Agave nectar

Coconut oil

Extra-virgin olive oil

Hemp milk (chocolate and vanilla)

Kombucha

Sea salt (Celtic, Hawaiian Red Alea)

Stone-ground mustard

Yoshida's teriyaki sauce

A FEW RECIPES

LAIRD: I've known for 8 years that my friend Giada De Laurentiis is a uniquely gifted cook, so I wasn't surprised when millions of others also responded to her talent. As host of the Food Network's hit show *Everyday Italian*, she creates dishes that are healthy, easy to make, and delicious—the ideal food trifecta. Here, she shares two recipes from her private stash.

GIADA: It's impressive to watch Laird eat. Of course, all athletes eat a lot—they need the energy—but he truly enjoys the process. As someone who loves to cook, I appreciate that. In keeping with his sport, both of my recipes have connections to the sea. Growing up, I spent a lot of time on the island of Capri, off the coast of Naples. Capri is known for its seafood; in particular, its array of fresh fish. I've had many grilled seafood salads there, and this is one of my favorites. People tend to think of salads as boring, but they're fantastic if you mix different textures: crunchy red peppers, creamy cannellini beans, chewy calamari, silky sea scallops.

GRILLED SEAFOOD SALAD
Recipe courtesy of Giada De Laurentiis

½ cup olive oil

2 cloves garlic, finely chopped

1 tablespoon chopped fresh flat-leaf parsley

1 teaspoon chopped fresh marjoram

1 teaspoon chopped fresh thyme

¼ cup fresh lemon juice (from about 1 lemon)

1 teaspoon salt + more to taste

1 teaspoon freshly ground black pepper + more to taste

12 ounces sea scallops

12 ounces cleaned squid, bodies only

1 can (15 ounces) white cannellini beans, rinsed and drained

3 ounces arugula leaves (about 6 cups)

2 carrots, peeled and cut into thin strips approximately 2" long

½ yellow bell pepper, cut into thin strips approximately 2" long

1 large head radicchio, leaves separated

In a small, heavy skillet, heat the oil over medium heat. Add the garlic, parsley, marjoram, and thyme and cook, stirring, for about 30 seconds, or until fragrant. Transfer to a small bowl and cool to room temperature. Whisk in the lemon juice and ½ teaspoon each of the salt and black pepper. Set aside.

Prepare a charcoal or gas grill for medium-high heat, or preheat a ridged grill pan over medium-high heat. Pat the scallops and squid dry with paper towels, brush them with 2 tablespoons of the reserved dressing, and sprinkle with remaining ½ teaspoon each of the salt and black pepper. Thread the scallops onto skewers and grill with the squid for about 2 minutes per side, or until just cooked through, turning once. Cool completely. Remove the scallops from the skewers and cut the squid crosswise into ¼"-wide rings.

In a large bowl, combine the beans, arugula, carrots, and bell pepper. Toss with enough of the reserved dressing to coat. Season with more salt and pepper to taste.

Place 1 large or 2 medium radicchio leaves on each of 4 plates. Spoon the bean salad into the radicchio cups and top with the scallops and squid. Drizzle with the remaining dressing and serve.

MAKES 4 SERVINGS

A few notes about this recipe:

- You can substitute any herbs you'd like in the dressing, but note that I don't use balsamic vinegar. It would break down the texture of the calamari and the scallops.

- Be careful: It's easy to overcook scallops.

- I think people are afraid of calamari (squid) sometimes, but at a good seafood store you can buy them already cleaned. All you have to do is slice them.

CAPONATA Recipe courtesy of Giada De Laurentiis

The caponata recipe originated aboard a boat in Santorini, Greece, where I shot a show. You could say it's a Greek interpretation of a classic Italian dish. Traditionally, caponata is a Sicilian relish made with eggplant, zucchini, and tomatoes, and they add vinegar and raisins. This version is loaded with vegetables, like a ratatouille.

> 1 can (14.5 ounces) diced tomatoes, with their juice
>
> 1 large Japanese eggplant, cut into 1" rounds
>
> 2 summer squash, cut into 1" rounds
>
> 2 zucchini, cut into 1" rounds
>
> 2 tomatoes, cut into wedges
>
> 1 red onion, peeled and cut into 1" wedges
>
> 1 potato, peeled and cut into 1" cubes
>
> 3 cloves garlic, minced
>
> ¼ cup extra-virgin olive oil
>
> 1½ teaspoons salt
>
> 1 teaspoon freshly ground black pepper
>
> 1 teaspoon dried oregano
>
> 4–6 slices toasted sourdough bread (optional, for main dish)

Preheat the oven to 400°F.

Pour the canned tomatoes into a 3½-quart baking dish and spread to cover the bottom. In a large bowl, combine the eggplant, squash, zucchini, fresh tomatoes, onion, potato, garlic, oil, salt, pepper, and oregano. Toss to coat.

Layer the vegetables on top of the canned tomatoes. Cover the baking dish with foil and bake for 20 minutes. Remove the foil and bake for another 30 to 40 minutes, or until the edges of the vegetables are golden.

Serve as a side dish, or spoon over toasted sourdough bread for a main dish.

MAKES 4 TO 6 SERVINGS

A few notes about this recipe:

✛ Notice that I cook this dish at a high temperature. If you let vegetables sit in the oven for a long time at low temperatures, they get soggy.

✛ Make sure you remove the foil after 20 minutes so the edges become golden brown.

✛ The potatoes add heartiness and creaminess. You don't have to cut carbs out of your life completely. The more you try to do that, the more you're going to crave them.

✛ I use Japanese eggplant so I don't have to worry about salting it and letting it sit. Also, it has a softer texture.

✛ One thing I love about this recipe is that I can make it the night before. It just gets better and better as it sits.

POISSON CRU

As if you needed another reason to go to Tahiti. This local dish is a kind of ceviche made with raw fish, lime, vegetables, and coconut milk. Every corner store and restaurant sells it, and it can be made in any number of variations. There's lots of chopping involved but no cooking. This is a classic recipe, with the most commonly used ingredients. Each time you make it, you can experiment with your own mix of seasonings.

$\frac{2}{3}$ cup coconut milk or cream

$\frac{1}{2}$ cup fresh lime juice

1 red onion, finely diced

1 large tomato, seeded and diced

1 small cucumber, peeled, seeded, and finely diced

2 carrots, finely diced

1 teaspoon grated lime zest

1 teaspoon sea salt

1 pound sushi-grade ahi tuna, cut into $\frac{1}{2}$" cubes

In a large glass bowl, combine the milk or cream, lime juice, onion, tomato, cucumber, carrots, lime zest, and salt. Add the tuna and let marinate for 15 minutes. Drain the excess liquid, transfer to 4 plates, and serve.

MAKES 4 SERVINGS

SIMPLE, DELUXE *FISH*

These fish recipes are two of the best I've eaten, and they're so easy to do. They come from my friends Brett Lickle and Nate Heydari, respectively. These are two guys who know fish: Nate owns my favorite sushi restaurant in Malibu, Bui Sushi; and as for Brett, his fishing skills are surpassed only by his surfing skills. Each of these is so easy to make that it's less a recipe than a strategy; the flavors taste great on their own, spectacular when combined. As always, the key is to get the freshest ingredients you can.

BRETT LICKLE'S RASPBERRY SALMON

2 tablespoons olive oil

4 wild salmon fillets (6–8 ounces each)

1 teaspoon sea salt

½ teaspoon cracked black pepper

2 cups fresh raspberries

1 tablespoon brown sugar

1 tablespoon honey

Preheat the oven to 350°F.

Coat the bottom of a large glass baking dish with the oil. Add the salmon and sprinkle with the salt and pepper. Let sit for 1 to 2 hours so the salt dissolves.

In a medium bowl, mash the raspberries, brown sugar, and honey together. Spread over the top of the salmon.

Bake for 10 minutes, or until the salmon is opaque in the center and flakes easily with a fork (the time will vary depending on the thickness of the fish). Increase the heat to broil, and broil the salmon for 1 to 2 minutes, or until the raspberries begin to bubble slightly. Serve hot.

MAKES 4 SERVINGS

NATE HEYDARI'S MANGO GINGER SALMON

2 cups diced mango
2/3 cup soy sauce
2 tablespoons minced fresh ginger
4 wild salmon fillets (6–8 ounces each)

Preheat the oven to 350°F.

In a large skillet, combine the mango, soy sauce, and ginger. Cook, stirring, over medium heat for about 3 minutes, or until the ginger is softened.

Place the salmon in a large glass baking dish. Pour the mango mixture over the salmon. Bake for 10 to 15 minutes, or until the salmon is opaque in the center and flakes easily with a fork (the time will vary depending on the thickness of the fish).

MAKES 4 SERVINGS

LAIRD'S FAVORITE MEAT LOAF Recipe courtesy of Gabrielle Reece

Laird's mother used to make this, so it's his nostalgic food. It's the easiest thing in the world to do. Adding the kale keeps the meat moist, but don't go crazy with the barbecue sauce or it will be too rich. Since the pan is lined with parchment, you can drain off the fat.

3 pounds ground beef (not the leanest kind; I like 80%)

1 pound ground organic, free-range turkey

2 cups canned corn niblets

2 cups grated Cheddar cheese

2 cups rolled oats

4 eggs, beaten

2 teaspoons sea salt

1 teaspoon freshly ground black pepper

1 tablespoon olive oil

1 large onion, diced

Parchment paper

1 bunch kale

3 tablespoons barbecue sauce or teriyaki sauce

Preheat the oven to 375°F.

In a large bowl, combine the beef, turkey, corn, cheese, oats, eggs, salt, and pepper. Do not overmix.

Heat the oil in a small skillet over medium heat. Add the onion and cook, stirring, for about 5 minutes, or just until softened. Add to the other ingredients and mix in.

Line a 9" × 13" baking pan with parchment paper. Transfer the meat mixture to the pan and pack densely (the mixture won't rise).

Peel the kale stems and place the kale over the top of the meat loaf so it forms a skin. Drizzle the barbecue sauce or teriyaki sauce over the top of the kale in a grid pattern. Bake for 1 hour 15 minutes, then remove from the oven and let sit in the pan for 30 minutes. Serve from the pan or transfer to a platter.

YIELD: 8 TO 10 SERVINGS

MY SMOOTHIE RECIPE

I like to start the day with this smoothie. Liquids are easier to digest than solids, so less than an hour after drinking this, I'm ready for whatever activity is on the agenda. The great thing about smoothies is that you can blend up your favorite mix of ingredients, flavors, and supplements, depending on what you're aiming for. This mix contains a huge amount of nutrients, and they're easily absorbed in liquid form—your body is less efficient at processing vitamins when you take a fistful of pills. For more information on these supplements, see page 114.

1 tablespoon Catie's Organic Greens
1 tablespoon Catie's Vitamin C Plus
1 scoop Neuro 1
2 scoops Muscle Milk protein powder
1 tablespoon Udo's Oil 3-6-9 Blend
1–2 frozen bananas
1 cup frozen berries (any kind; I like blueberries, boysenberries, strawberries, raspberries, or blackberries)
½ cup organic apple or cherry juice or hemp milk (see page 116)
½ cup filtered water

Put all of the ingredients in a blender and mix at ice-crushing speed for 30 seconds. For a lighter version, eliminate the juice (or hemp milk) and substitute an additional ½ cup water, reduce the protein powder to 1 scoop, and use just 1 teaspoon oil and half of a frozen banana.

141

Water always finds the path of least resistance. It flows. You never see square turns on a river. There's always a curvature. I think life's like that, too. It has a natural curve, an arc. I think it's our job to trust in that. So you could say that I believe in things being predestined. How could I not? When I think of my life, I feel as though I've always been given the absolute right circumstances to help create who I am. If I hadn't grown up in Hawaii, cut my teeth at Pipeline, and been surrounded by the era's greatest surfers throughout my childhood, I don't know where I would have ended up. And I don't want to know. I'm grateful for all of the twists and turns of fate that have brought me here.

PART 3

SOUL

As long as you think that you're somehow in control of everything, you're always going to be struggling and striving. That's the opposite of letting things flow. Ask any martial arts master: The power isn't found in resistance. Strength comes from yielding to what is. Counterintuitive though it may be, fighting puts you in a weaker position.

Instead of trying to enjoy our lives more, or pursuing the idea of getting into the position someday of being able to enjoy our lives more—maybe we should just start enjoying! Right this moment. What if you dared to accept that much of what happens is out of your hands and trusted in life to unfold in a perfect way? Then you could sit back, look out at the horizon, and relax.

WHAT MATTERS

TO FIND YOUR PASSION, YOU HAVE TO LOOK INWARD. IF YOU LOOK OUTWARD, ALL YOU'LL SEE IS WHAT OTHER PEOPLE ARE DOING. YOU'RE NOT OTHER PEOPLE.

ONE SET OF FOOTPRINTS

I remember when I was a kid growing up in Kauai, a teacher asked me what I wanted to do with my life. Obviously, she didn't like my answer (to surf) because I also remember her shaking her head and telling me, "You can't eat your surfboard." Well, I've been doing that for a while now, and at this point it tastes pretty good. Maybe she was waiting for me to say, "Oh, you're right. I'll be a lawyer." That would have been a very long wait.

The point is: Your path is yours alone. And if it's the path less traveled, that's absolutely fine. The world doesn't need more conformists. The world needs more people who create and question and search. If you don't fit in, celebrate that, and then get ready to stand your ground. Our society has some rigid roles for people, and when you decide that you don't want to play the same game as everyone else, you might not get much support for your decision. Don't let that discourage you. The best way to find your path is to start with a dream and then refuse to listen to anyone else's opinions about what you "can" and "can't" do in pursuit of that dream.

My spiritual beliefs have helped me walk the path that I knew I needed to be on. I've been reading the Bible since I was 16, when I first discovered it (through a girl I was dating—how else?). I've always found something golden and truthful in its pages. That doesn't mean I'm running around pushing it on other people or saying, "Why aren't you in church?" Ultimately, my belief is that there's a bigger belief than any single religion contains. Most intelligent people I've met believe in something larger than themselves. They might not call it God or Buddha or Muhammad; they might say it's the oceans or the trillions of stars in the sky. But aside from haggling over the description and the name and the title, we realize that there's something going on that orchestrated all of this and that we're not just here as a matter of coincidence. Whatever you believe in, let that be your source of strength.

I believe that our imagination is our connection to higher knowledge. It's the most formidable tool that we have, an amazing source of inspiration. And then, of course, there's the world we live in, which is no slouch in that area, either. What we've been given here is precious: majestic in its smallest details and its grandest spectacles. Anytime you feel like you're in danger of forgetting that, I recommend taking a good look at a 50-foot wave. Anyone who can be around something that powerful and not feel humbled has some serious analyzing to do. You can't deny the spiritual world when you're staring into its eyes.

LIFE LESSONS

THERE ARE TWO WAYS TO LEARN SOMETHING:
THE EASY WAY AND THE HARD WAY. LIKE MOST
PEOPLE, I'VE HAD MY SHARE OF THE HARD WAY.
AND ALSO LIKE MOST PEOPLE, MY LIFE PHILOSOPHY
IS A WORK IN PROGRESS. BUT FOR WHAT IT'S WORTH,
THESE ARE A FEW THINGS THAT I'VE COME TO BELIEVE.

✦ **YOU REAP WHAT YOU SOW** I think of myself as Instant Karma Guy. The feedback I get is almost always immediate. I say something snotty; 5 seconds later, I stub my toe. It's cause and effect. Ebb and flow. Put it out there; you'll get it back. If you wake up in a bad mood, then you'll be given reasons to be in a bad mood. If you're stressed, you'll get stress. If you're satisfied, you'll be given satisfaction. People don't always have an awareness of karma. They'll say, "Oh, poor me, what did I do to deserve *that*?" I'll tell you what: something. At the end of the day, everything's math.

✦ **UNDERSTAND THAT YOU CAN'T ALWAYS UNDERSTAND** Everything has a purpose. The formula may not be $1 + 1 = 2$. It may not be a formula we understand at all. But it's still a formula. I truly believe that everything's going according to plan— but it's out of our hands. When it comes to my own life, I know I'm just holding on for the ride. In hindsight, there's great evidence of that. But along the way, especially when the water gets rough, it can be hard to believe it. I don't always get what I want—no one does. There have been days when I've missed epic swells or giant snowfalls because I've been down-on-the-floor sick. When that happens, it's torture; more than anything, I want to be out there surfing or snowboarding. But I've learned to accept that on some days I'm not meant to. Ultimately, I think the best way to take advantage of what life has to offer is to be open to whatever comes, even when it doesn't arrive in the exact package you envisioned. No, there's no hard proof that everything's unfolding as it should. But that's what faith is: belief without proof.

⊹ IF YOU'RE NOT PREPARED, DON'T BE SURPRISED IF YOU FAIL At the end of the day, it's about doing the work. If you haven't ridden your bike very much, you can't expect to race up l'Alpe-d'Huez. Again, it's cause and effect. This is a truth that sometimes gets lost. Our society holds that you can take a pill to lose weight or become happy or get healthy; that gratification should be instant; that a crash course can substitute for a thorough education. As a result, many people believe that they don't have to do anything all that hard. Wrong. Pure magic can happen, of course, but far more often, luck is the result of elbow grease. That said, nobody's lucky all the time. When you do fail, instead of being depressed about it, use it as an opportunity for reflection. What didn't work? Why? What could you do differently next time?

⊹ COMPLAINING IS A LUXURY When I was 11, my mother took me to India and Afghanistan. Her intent was to expose me to other cultures to make me appreciate how abundant and affluent things are here. And it worked. I remember seeing a lone nomad walking through the middle of a barren desert—a hundred miles from nowhere—and he had only one arm. He was a banished one, and he was out there fending for himself. You see something like that and it pretty much shuts down the impulse to whine. Everything's relative. All these things you think are so irksome in your life—the report that's due, the nasty thing your neighbor said, that the restaurant overcooked your porterhouse—you wouldn't even notice them unless everything else was fine. When you're hurt or sick or worried about someone you love, then things like that have no relevance. You learn very quickly what matters. So the next time you hear yourself complaining, remember how fortunate you are.

❖ **USE WORDS WISELY** There's something to the adage that if you can't say something nice, then don't say anything. There are times when it's better to keep quiet. People have a difficult time with that. It's hard for humans not to flap. We just like to talk. And people like negative talk about others because it makes them feel better. But the best gossip is no gossip.

Minding your own business is an undervalued skill. There is, however, an exception to that rule: When you see somebody doing something and you sense that they might get hurt as a result of it, speak up. If you don't, you'll regret it. As much as voicing your opinion might offend them, that's nothing compared to how you'll feel if you keep quiet and something happens to them.

❖ **HAPPINESS IS EASIER (AND SMARTER)** I read somewhere that it takes 43 muscles to frown and 17 to smile. If that's true, then it's actually easier to be happy than it is to be unhappy. Why, then, does it sometimes seem as though everybody's miserable? Personally, I tell myself that there's no time for wallowing on the downside. Life is just not that long. If you just had a really good time until the finale, how bad could that be? I think the key to happiness is maximizing each day. So if you're unhappy, here's a simple prescription: Live harder.

❖ **EMBRACE THE NEW** Novelty is the antidote to boredom, but we tend to get comfortable with what we know—and as the rut deepens, fresh experiences are even less welcome. We all know people who seem old even if they aren't. Discovering new things keeps you young. It's about expanding your horizons. If you stop exploring, everything becomes smaller. I think that the more texture you can have in your life, the better. A simple way to do this is by embracing new things: music, sports, ideas, anything.

✥ ENJOY CREATION If all you did in your lifetime was enjoy the beautiful things around you—the sunset, moon, and clouds or all the plants and animals—that would be a worthy life. Because I spend so much time in the ocean and outside in general, I've seen some of nature's more radical spectacles. I've been surrounded by—literally— thousands of dolphins. I've seen a double rainbow that formed two perfect concentric circles. I've flown inside a hurricane. But all of nature's creations are worth taking the time to admire. The "ordinary" is not really ordinary at all. In Maui I have two pet razorback pigs, Ginger and Marianne. They're amazing animals, perfect in every detail. Every time I look at them, I have to smile. And it's like that all around us. Nature's genius is everywhere, and though it might sound obvious, I think that all of us could do a better job of appreciating it.

MY MOTHER, MY HERO

JoAnn Zerfas was a one-of-a-kind woman who passed away far too early, at 53, of a brain aneurysm. She was an awesome parent, a fiercely loving spirit, and the single biggest influence on my life.

✥ My mom had a great imagination, and she encouraged me to use mine, too; she read me all kinds of fantastical books, like *Lord of the Rings* and *Dune*. In general, she was a heavy cultivator of dreaming. And I believe that all the things I've done in my life—the houses I've built, the waves I've ridden, becoming a husband and a father—have been a result of being able to imagine them first. That's her legacy.

✥ She had an iron core of ethics and morals. One thing she instilled in me when I was young was that you can be anything you want to be and do anything you want to do—as long as you're not hurting anyone else. She used to sing the song that went, "Be kind to your web-footed friends, for a duck may be somebody's mother."

✥ When I was 10, she took me out of school, and we went across Europe and through Afghanistan and India. I had my 11th birthday in Kabul. I remember being told that they didn't understand the concept of birthdays. Instead they would ask, "How many moons are you?" Mom wanted to expose me to other places in the world. Mission accomplished. How many 11-year-olds do you know who've been to the Khyber Pass in winter?

✥ She was a relentless worker. Unbelievable energy. Her nickname was Jetty, as in "jet airplane," because she was always on the move. She would literally work 16 hours a day, no problem, and she'd keep that up 7 days a week.

✥ She was a sentimental person. Family was everything. We always celebrated birthdays and holidays. I think the first time I didn't come home for Christmas, I was in my thirties. You were home for the holidays. That's just the way it was.

✥ Kauai was her place. She came and never left. She had found where she wanted to be. She appreciated the beauty of nature and the ocean.

✥ No matter how dilapidated the house was—and I'm talking outhouses and cold showers—Mom kept everything meticulously clean. Our clothes were always clean. You could eat off the floor in our house. I don't know how there were enough hours in the day for her to do everything that she did.

✥ In the late '70s, she started a helicopter touring company on Kauai called Papillon. She'd been taken on a flight by Red Johnson, a retired air force pilot who lived on the island, and after that the two of them collaborated—he did the flights, and she created the infrastructure. Her organizational skills made her a natural for business. And she loved it. She just immersed herself. It was the first time in her life she had the opportunity to explore a career—she was 20 when I was born, so she'd started her family young. She had such a passion for helicopters. Papillon eventually grew into the largest helicopter touring company in the state of Hawaii.

✥ You wouldn't play Scrabble with my mom. She was supersmart, and she'd read the dictionary, like, three times. You didn't play word games against her, and you didn't argue with her. Mom would have made a great litigator.

✥ She wasn't scared of anybody. Nobody. I don't care if you're 10 feet tall and the meanest guy on the planet. Mom would walk right up into your face if you did something wrong to her or her family. She'd come all guns blazing. I remember one time in Kauai when two guys had a fight in our driveway. They were some gnarly characters. Mom came down and was just livid, and they cursed at her and made threats. Later that day the elder of the area made them come back to the house and apologize. Because she was above reproach.

⚜ She was just a really loving person. People used to come to Mom all the time. She was always counseling people—men and women. As a parent, she was supercool. She was open to trying to understand the difficulties of being a kid and the frustrations of being a teenager. No matter what, she was always positive.

⚜ Her favorite thing was to look for seashells. She absolutely loved that. I spent a lot of time with her picking up shells on the beach while I was growing up. She'd display them in jars, bowls, cases—it was an epic collection.

⚜ We sprinkled her ashes over the Na Pali Coast of Kauai. It was a nine-helicopter procession. She'd died suddenly, but even so, she'd left specific instructions as to exactly how she wanted things to be and that all of her organs were to be donated. That was Mom, helping people and organized to the end, down to dotting the last *i*.

FAMILY MATTERS

RAISING KIDS IS THE ULTIMATE JOURNEY, AND I FEEL INCREDIBLY LUCKY TO BE ON IT. IT'S HUMBLING— AND GRATIFYING BEYOND WORDS—TO BE A PARENT. GABBY AND I DON'T CLAIM TO BE CHILD-RAISING EXPERTS; WHAT SEEMS TO WORK FOR US IS TO BE AUTHENTICALLY OURSELVES. EVERY PARENT HAS HIS OR HER OWN SET OF PHILOSOPHIES, DISCOVERIES, AND STRATEGIES. HERE ARE SOME OF OURS.

GABBY: We only have girls around here: Izabela, 13; Reece, 5; and Brody, 1. We're balancing out the testosterone.

When I became a mother, I wasn't nervous. You're *in* it. You do feel as though you don't know what you're doing. Then, all of sudden, that stops. The bottom line is that you do the best you can.

LAIRD: People always ask how having children affects my thinking about what I do in terms of the risks that I take. I've thought about the answer a lot. I want people to value me for who I am, and the ocean *is* who I am. I brought my kids into the world—they didn't ask to be born—but it seems to me to be wrong if I stop being myself because of them. It'd almost be cheating them.

GABBY: You always want to make sure your children are safe, but when you're too fearful, you're going to pass that on to them. I think it's important for them to stay joyous and not become overly fearful themselves.

So much of parenting is consistency. It's like any relationship in that regard.

LAIRD: We're not Little League parents. I think it would be unbelievably sad to make your kids do something you want to do. We're just going to provide opportunity and create exposure: Here's windsurfing, here's snowboarding, here's film, here's scholarship, here are books, here's golf. It's whatever they want to do. The primary objective is to create a fulfilled person.

GABBY: I'll let Reece eat cake and ice cream. I don't want to make them issues or taboos. I'll let her explore things. She doesn't drink soda, though. I think if you can avoid that, you should.

LAIRD: The most important thing you can do is give all your love and lots of your time to your kids. Give them grown-up answers to their questions. Exercise patience and tolerance like you never knew you had. And always remember that your children owe you nothing. You, on the other hand, owe them everything.

DON WILDMAN

I met Don Wildman in 1995 on a heli-snowboarding trip in British Columbia. We hit if off immediately, though I don't think either of us suspected that we would play such a major role in one another's lives. In fact, we didn't keep in touch after the trip, and it wasn't until 2 years later that our paths crossed again. I'd just moved to Malibu, and one day I walked into Coogies, a local restaurant, and there was Don, drinking an espresso in his mountain bike gear.

I knew he was an accomplished athlete and that, along with being an expert snowboarder, he'd competed in the Hawaiian Ironman Triathlon nine times, ridden his bike in the 3,000-mile Race Across America, and won many of sailing's most prestigious events. I also knew that he had retired from an extremely successful career after founding the chain of health clubs that became Bally Total Fitness. What I didn't know was that Don, who recently celebrated his 75th birthday, would also become the toughest training partner I've ever had.

Since then, during the past decade, we've

had countless cups of espresso together; spent thousands of hours in the water, on the slopes, on the trails, and in the gym. We've gone on adventures in Alaska, Argentina, New Zealand, Canada, Europe, and Indonesia; we've paddled through the Grand Canyon on the Colorado River and across the Hawaiian Islands chain. He's taught me everything he knows about mountain biking (which is a lot), and I've taught him about surfing and paddling. He also introduced me to the Circuit, a weight-lifting routine that he spent decades fine-tuning (see page 47).

Don is gung ho in the purest sense. If I called him up in the middle of the night and said, "Hey Don, let's go paddle the Nile" or "Look, there's this thing I want to do in the Arctic," he'd say, "I'm there. I'll pack right now. We'll catch a plane in the morning." Don is one of the great bad-asses of all time. He's also one of the smartest, most generous, most supportive guys you could ever meet.

Here are some words of wisdom from Don Wildman, my friend and inspiration. As you'll see, he knows a thing or two about life.

- I have a house on the beach at Malibu. I have a lot of fancy neighbors, but they're never at the beach. We're the only ones out there. So are we wrong, or is everybody else wrong? I think everybody else is wrong. I think we've got it right; we're sitting on surfboards looking at the coastline and saying, "Hey, life is unbelievable." I don't know what the rest of the world is doing, but I think we got it figured out right here, right now.
- I remember the first football game I played in high school. We were behind; I was supposed to catch the kick shot. The pressure . . . If I fumbled, we would lose the game. I caught it, and I still remember all the noise, the fans yelling. And I thought to myself, *This is great! This is amazing!* And I still have that feeling about competition. I love it.
- I've done the Hawaiian Ironman Triathlon nine times. The first time I did it was something of a lark. I wasn't even worrying about finishing. I got to the finish line, and they told me I'd won! I couldn't believe it. But then they found this Canadian guy who beat me by a

(continued)

minute or so. I went back the next year, and he beat me again. Heck of a runner. I ultimately beat him after 8 years.

⚜ I think one of the reasons I train is because it makes you mentally tough in all areas of your life, including business. It teaches you discipline, having to do things you don't particularly want to do every day—but you find the determination to stay motivated. Basically, anything that doesn't kill you makes you stronger.

⚜ Everything I do, I overdo.

⚜ One of the scariest things I've done is the Aspen downhill. I was the oldest competitor by 30 years. My son convinced me that it would be really fun. The night before the race, for the first time in my life, I dreamt that I'd died. Next morning I got up, put on the skintight outfit, the helmet, the whole thing. The race was terrifying. The amount of force downhill puts on your legs is unbelievable. One girl broke her jaw; one guy broke his leg. I got to the finish line, and I said, "How'd I do? Did I break the record?"

because I thought I was so out of control. And they said, "No, you were the slowest." So I went back up and did it again. And the second time I beat one guy.

⚜ Some people have to win. I don't have to win. I really like to win, and I'll do my level best to figure out how to win. But if I lose, it doesn't totally destroy me. It makes me want to try harder.

⚜ My father gave me some simple advice once. He said, "When you're doing something, run. Rather than walk, you run." Everyone thinks it's so hard to get ahead, but it's not, because most people are lazy.

⚜ Sixty years ago there was an adage that too much exercise would give you an "athlete's heart." The professionals were telling people, "If you overexercise, it's very dangerous because you will enlarge your heart and you will die." Also, everyone was told that if you worked out with weights it would make you muscle-bound. In the early days of the health club business, that was my number one bugaboo in getting women to join the gym. The first thing out of their mouths was "I don't want to get muscles." And it was so absurd, like, "What do you want, fat?" There are only two choices.

- You can't beat age. But you can certainly slow it down.
- As you get older, it takes you longer to recover from training, and you've got to avoid injuries. But one thing's for sure: Activity is the key ingredient. When people stop moving, that's when it's all over. The other part of aging well is mental, being happy and having the right attitude. Whatever you're doing, I think you need to find it fun.

In athletics, most people have been programmed to believe that once you get into your late twenties, it's all over for you. That's totally crazy. People at any age can be competitive. You just have to have the ambition and the desire.

- Living a great life is not about how much money you have. It's about how good you are at maximizing each day.
- You have to embrace change. Because no matter what we're doing today that we think is so fantastic, there's gonna be a better way to do it in the near future. And I always want to be on that edge. I don't care how old I am, I want to be among the first people doing something.
- If the brain stays young, you'll stay young.

THE CROSSINGS

WHEN I LEARNED THAT MY CLOSE FRIEND'S SON HAD AUTISM, I WANTED TO DO SOMETHING TO HELP.

A PATH OF PURPOSE I've been working with photographer Don King since the earliest days of my career. Over the years, we've made several films together and shared more adventures than I can count, ranging from laid-back fun to off-the-charts intense. His talent is astonishing. You can put Don into the craziest situation on the biggest, most furious day, with 70-foot waves breaking everywhere, and he's like an oasis of calm. He takes beautiful pictures in even the most treacherous conditions. As a former champion swimmer, he understands water. When he's in the ocean he's at home, and he captures that deeper understanding in his images. The only thing better than working with Don has been getting to know him and his family personally.

Don and his wife, Julianne, have three boys: Aikau, Dane, and their youngest son, Beau. As an infant and then a toddler, Beau was a happy, sociable kid. But suddenly, sometime between Beau's second and third birthday, he changed. It was as though, as Don describes it, the lights went out. Beau became silent and withdrawn, wouldn't make eye contact. The Kings took him to the doctor, but the tests came back normal. Meanwhile, Beau kept getting worse. It was only after they'd seen several more doctors that Don and Julianne were given a diagnosis: Beau was autistic.

They launched themselves into learning everything they possibly could about the disease, determined to find the right course of action and, ultimately, a solution. But nothing about autism is that cut-and-dried. Even its definition is a generalization: a complex developmental disorder that causes problems with social interaction and communication. What that means is as varied as the number of kids afflicted with it. The world Don and Julianne encountered—doctors, other parents, autistic kids—was a maze of contradictions and unsolved mysteries.

No one, it seemed, knew much for sure about autism except for two things: First, the number of autistic children in the United States is skyrocketing; today, in 2008, one in every 150 children has the disease, with boys four times more susceptible than girls. A new case of autism is diagnosed every 20 minutes. The other accepted fact is that many autistic kids have high levels of heavy metals in their bodies, especially mercury.

They also found a reason for hope: Some children recover. As the Kings dedicated their lives to helping their son, they decided to chronicle the journey. When I heard they'd begun to make a film, *Beautiful Son,* I wanted to help them raise the money to complete it. I'd been thinking about doing a series of manual-powered channel crossings, cycling and standup paddling from point A to point B in various parts of the world, and I realized that tackling these challenges with a purpose would make them even better. And so we set out to make that happen.

The first crossing I did was in June 2006, from London to Paris, riding from London to Dover, paddling across the English Channel, and then picking up my bike again on the French shore to end at the Arc de Triomphe. The 265-mile journey took 2 days—2 long days. The weather was stormy and rainy, and the English Channel, a body of water that's rough on the calmest days, was at its nastiest. Conditions were tough, even for the crew. But we raised more than $100,000, and, equally as important, we raised awareness.

The following summer, Dave Kalama and I tackled the second stage of our crossing fund-raisers, traversing 500 miles through the Hawaiian Island chain from the Big Island all the way to Kauai. You've heard of the TV show *Hawaii Five-O*? Well, I like to call this crossing "Hawaii Five-Uh-Oh." In a word, it was hard. We pedaled our bikes across the islands and standup paddled across the channels between them. It took us 5 days. I don't think either of us will ever forget it—especially the 79-mile paddle across the Kaieiewaho Channel between Oahu and Kauai.

It was the last leg of the whole journey, and it would've been the hardest even under the best conditions. With Kona winds blowing hard in our faces and thunderstorms flashing along the way, we certainly didn't have them. At times Dave and I felt as though we were trying to climb Everest on a day when we should've stayed in our tents. That crossing alone took us 20 hours. Strangely, though it was the most difficult thing that either of us had ever done, we never seriously entertained the notion of quitting. There's power in thinking about those who are struggling with something far more significant, such as autism.

In October 2007, Don and Julianne's film, *Beautiful Son*, debuted at the Hawaii International Film Festival, where it won the prize for Best Documentary. They continue to do everything possible to help Beau. He has good days and not-so-good days. For my part, I hope to see the day when no family has to endure this pain. Until then, Dave and I will continue to make these crossings. I remember the dawn on that last day, after grinding all night toward Kauai, when I first spotted land. My immediate thought was: *It's still so far away.* But once I saw it, I knew we would get there. Until there's an end in sight to this particular journey—the quest to cure this disease—we'll be paddling as hard as we can.

ON THE OCEAN

I NEED THE OCEAN. YOU NEED THE OCEAN. AND MEANWHILE, THE OCEAN ALSO NEEDS US.

THE BLUE PLANET BLUES Water is the essence of life. Our planet's made of water. We're made of water. Our blood contains the same trace minerals as seawater, only in slightly different proportions. The oceans cover more than three-quarters of the earth's surface, provide 50 percent of our oxygen, and are home to more than 80 percent of all known life forms. As a species, we're connected to this realm; and for me, personally, it also serves as both my workplace and my inspiration. I'm dependent on the ocean to bring me fulfillment, challenge, and all the things that make up who I am. I need to spend a certain amount of time alone, and I get that in the water. The ocean gives me solitude—there's no access; no one can get to you there. At times I feel as though I belong out there more than I belong on land. And anyone else who feels the same way, who loves the ocean, is a friend of mine.

Unfortunately—and it's becoming more obvious every day—we're doing a terrible job of taking care our waters. Whether it's by polluting them with chemicals and plastics or by overfishing or by unraveling the web of life by exterminating species—the list goes on. The really crazy part about all this is that we're the ones who will pay for it. We mess with the oceans at our peril.

We know pathetically little about how the oceans work in the larger scheme of the earth. We've discovered that they control our climate, but we don't understand exactly how; we know that the depths are vast, but we've explored only a fraction of them. One thing we do know is that the ocean can—and does—unleash a tremendous amount of power. Anyone who didn't already know how strong these forces are witnessed it firsthand in 2004 when the tsunami hit Indonesia. And again in 2005, during Hurricane Katrina. But it shouldn't take something so extreme before we respect the waters that surround us.

On some days I feel more hopeful than others, but there aren't too many signs of things changing for the better. I'm thinking about Japanese fishermen rounding up dolphins in a cove in Taiji, Japan, and slaughtering them until the water is bright red with their blood. Apparently they kill hundreds every year because they consider dolphins to be pests who eat fish, stealing their livelihood. There's been some news coverage of that, at least, thanks to Australian surfer Dave Rastovich, the American actress Hayden Panettiere, and their friends, who paddled out to try to surround a pod before a fishing boat got to it. The boat beat them. Hopefully, others felt the same outrage that I did when I saw it.

Dolphins are magnificent creatures. Whenever I see them when I'm in the water, that's a good day in my book. I've watched dolphins do astonishing things, and I'm convinced that we know very little about them. There is no possible justification for what the Japanese are doing in that cove. And they know it—the place is cordoned off with barbed wire. They would really prefer that you don't know the first thing about it. That kind of insensitivity, that arrogant disrespect for life—are we, as custodians of this place, going to let that be our legacy?

There's another book's (at least) worth of stories to be told about the harm that's being done to sea creatures. But here's another concern. When I'm in California and I go out paddling in the morning, it never takes too long before I come across a floating plastic bag. I'll pick it up, and then I'll fill it with all the garbage that I find along the way. When I get back to shore, I always have a batch of trash with me. And that's just in a 3-mile radius. If you consider the entire coast, it's hard to imagine what's floating out there. But it's not the larger stuff that's the worst. As much of a blight as that is, if you can see it, you can clean it up. It's the stuff you *can't* see that really scares me. These disintegrating plastics and other debris degrade into a stew of toxic chemicals with names you can't pronounce, that do harm we can't even conceive of.

As humans with all this power, we think of ourselves as having dominion over the earth. The truth is, in the whole scheme of life, we really aren't in control of that much. Yes, we have these great heavy things we can do, but we are still at the mercy of much larger forces. It's the same with everything—large or small. Anything you don't respect, don't be surprised if it bites you hard one day. In the end, the ocean is going to take care of itself. It will have the last say.

A MAINLANDER'S GUIDE TO HAWAIIAN WISDOM

A *PLACE* WITH *SOUL* Yes, Hawaii is the 50th state, but after having spent my life there, I'd argue that it's only part of America on paper. The real Hawaii is a primal, magical place with a spirit all its own. Not only is it unlike any other state, it's unlike any place on earth. If you don't believe me, visit and see for yourself. And when you do, here are a few things you should know.

ALOHA

It means "hello"; it means "good-bye." And it also means something far more significant than either of those two words. There's a depth to "aloha" that isn't easily described because it encompasses an attitude toward life. If a Hawaiian tells you that you have aloha, that's the ultimate compliment. It's a spirit of grace, generosity, peace—a kind of spiritual check-list of all that's good. *Ha* in Hawaiian means "breath," and *aloha*'s literal meaning is "to breathe life." To have aloha means to share your life energy with others and with all that surrounds you. So how do you get some aloha? By being aware of everyone and everything that's around you, by caring about it all, and—to cut to the chase—by being cool. You'll know it when you feel it, and my advice is to feel it as often as you can.

MANA

Mana is similar to our concept of charisma, except the Hawaiians believe that it resides in the natural world as well as in people. For instance, on the island of Kauai, where I spent most of my childhood, everything is alive: the sky and the sea and the land. Even the rocks are alive. It's like nature on steroids: Everything's just busting out of the earth. To the Hawaiians, that aliveness—or mana—is the greatest source of power. Strength from rocks.

You can feel the mana all over the islands, but in my opinion it's especially strong in Kauai. It's the oldest part of the Hawaiian chain and the only island that was never conquered. If there really was a Garden of Eden, I can easily imagine it being there. Kauai has a vibe all its own, almost as if there's more oxygen in the air. When you fly over, coming from the land of Wal-Mart and Pizza Hut into a land of rivers, mountains, waterfalls, and ocean, it feels like shock therapy. You know that you're in a place where many before you have walked on those roads and ridden those waves. According to the concept of mana, everything has a spirit form—but some spots and some people have more than others. Set your radar on high, and you'll be able to feel it. We all can, but we tend to forget that. Some of the ways to increase your own mana, the Hawaiians believe, are by practicing long, deep breathing; spending more time in nature; and nourishing yourself with good food and exercise.

TI LEAVES

On the days when Pe'ahi is going off so big you can feel the ground shaking 5 miles away, we take a ti leaf with us when we go out to surf. The ti is a special leaf that the ancient Polynesians took on their voyages: You bring the leaf from the shore because the leaf will bring you back to shore. The ti, which is part of the lily family, is a sacred plant. It's believed to protect against evil spirits and is often placed in, and planted around, people's homes to encourage good fortune. I always thought I didn't have superstitions, but it turns out that I do. This is one of them.

AUMAKUA

Every Hawaiian has his own personal spirit guide, known as an *aumakua*. It's a protective force that often takes the form of an animal; three common aumakua are sharks, sea turtles, and owls. They're thought to embody the spirits of an individual's ancestors, and so it is considered very bad form (not to mention an invitation to bad luck) to eat or harm your aumakua. And conversely, it's considered a good omen whenever you see one, either in reality or in your dreams. My family isn't Hawaiian so we don't have an official aumakua, but if I were to choose one now, I think I'd go for the dolphin.

HAOLE

When I tell you that this word literally translates to "foreigner," I'm speaking from experience. As the only blond, non-Hawaiian kid in my school in Kauai, I was branded a haole from Day One. It meant that I did a lot of fighting. In time, I earned my acceptance among the locals, but I've never forgotten what it felt like to be treated as an unwelcome outsider.

Over the years, I've come to realize that there's also a larger and subtler meaning to "haole." It's not a skin color, it's a brain process. It really means someone whose mind-set is foreign—who behaves in a clueless manner. If you're unaware and disrespectful of your surroundings, you can devolve into a haole anywhere, anytime. It's all in your attitude.

I make my living as a surfer, but I would never call it a job. I'm not even sure you can think of it purely as sport. Surfing is a bigger concept. It's the essential element of my life, and if I had to compare it to anything, I'd say that surfing is like playing music. There can be endless variations on a song; infinite ways to make a melody. And likewise, everyone who rides a wave brings something unique to the process. No two people surf the same way, and no two waves are alike. It's a constant interpretation of whatever the ocean brings combined with whatever you bring. Surfing is motion, and its rhythm

PART 4
SURFING

and your approach to it should express who you are. Ride a longboard, a shortboard, a skimboard—any kind of board at all.

At the same time, conscious surfers understand that there's something deeply humbling at work. We're all equal before a wave. The wind, the tides, the pulse of the swell, the rhythms of the ocean, all went into creating its power. The best riders are attuned to every nuance of their environment. If you don't understand the wave, you can't respect it. And if you don't have respect, it's only a matter of time before the ocean teaches you to get some. Surfing connects you to nature, it brings you into this moment, and it challenges you. Those are far more important things than "Hey, you shred!"

PRIVATE LESSONS

Though there are obviously levels of skill in anything you do, the only wrong way to surf is if you're not having a good time. Yes, surfing can be a challenging sport— but only if you want it to be. Whether you're a pro or a novice, when you're on a wave, you leave the cares of the world behind. Depending on what level you're at, here are some things you want to think about.

BEGINNERS: *THE WATER'S EDGE* Everybody thinks

the most important part of surfing is some technical move you make on the board, like learning how to carve a turn or do a cutback or whatever. Wrong. The most important skill for anyone who wants to surf is to be comfortable in the ocean. And not just on a nice day. What happens when you find yourself tangled up in the whitewater, which can happen on even the smallest wave? Do you panic—or is it fun? You want to be relaxed and confident in turbulent conditions, so before you even think about buying a board, the first order of business is to become a strong swimmer. No swimming, no surfing.

One way to work on your swimming skills while becoming more acquainted with waves and how they behave is to spend some time bodysurfing. It's the purest, simplest thing: just you and the water. If you're sensitive to what's going on, you'll be able to feel the energy of the wave and learn how and where it breaks. Go somewhere with a sandy bottom, practice diving beneath the waves, and find out what it feels like to get hit by them. Watch other people doing it, get some fins, and play around.

Once you've done that groundwork—you're at home in the water, you understand where the current is, you've got some idea of how the waves work—then you can start thinking about a board. Start with a boogie board. After you've ridden some small waves on it, get yourself a surfboard.

Initially, I recommend something like one of those soft-top longboards so that when you get hit by it, you don't get hurt. It's discouraging to go out for the first time and get whacked in the head or split your lip open—and it happens. That's what the soft tops are for—so that your experience is a less damaging one.

Next, go to a place where there are other people in the water bodysurfing, boogie boarding, or surfing. Watch how they make their way out through the surf break and how they paddle to catch a wave. Notice what happens when they make a mistake. Study how they pop up onto their boards once they're on the wave. Before you even get into the water, try popping up on the sand. When you do that, you'll know right away what stance you are (which foot leads and which foot trails). One way will feel totally comfortable, and the other way will feel like you've got your hands tied behind your back. If you're a regular stance, your right foot will be back. If you're goofy, it will be your left. Another way to find out what someone's stance is, is to have them stand with their feet parallel and then push them. Whatever foot they put back first to steady themselves, that's their stance. And 90 percent of everyone will put the same foot back every time if they're allowing it to happen naturally.

Ideally, when you're starting out, you'll have access to well-shaped small waves that break over a sandy bottom. Waikiki's a good example of this. The best places for learning are shallow because that means the waves can break over a long distance. If the bottom changes abruptly from deep to shallow, then the waves break faster, and that makes things harder. One thing you want to remember if you're surfing in shallow water is to land flat when you fall. Lead with your butt. Sit back on your board. I call it an elegant dismount.

INTERMEDIATES: IN THE WAVES Once you can get up

on your board and ride small waves, it's time to refine your board. A good transition would be to swap the soft top for a similar-shaped board that's made out of an epoxy or fiberglass. You might consider a type of board known as a mini tanker, which is really a downsized longboard, about 8 or 9 feet long (longboards are defined by their nose shape, which is round). As far as fin configuration goes, I think it's good to learn on a single fin. You're going to be riding flat; you're not going to be on your edges that much when you're learning. Single fins are faster, and they teach you good foundational skills.

Probably the most counterproductive thing that people do when they're learning is to go out and get pro equipment. They'll look at the magazines and see Kelly Slater and Andy Irons riding little 6-foot boards that it's taken them 20 years to perfect. They're the best in the world; they can ride these things that are hard to paddle, hard to get up on, and need very aggressive waves to work functionally, among other issues. Things like the soft top and mini tanker, while they might not be what you consider "cool," are making it much easier for people to learn. People fall victim to getting an expert's equipment and not using the beginner stuff. Get over that, and learn how to surf.

Once you can ride a wave going straight, the next step is making a turn. Turning comes from your hips and shoulders. What you do is lead with whatever hand you have forward. If you're a regular foot, your left hand's forward; if you're a goofy foot, your right hand's forward. Put your hand straight out and have it lead you. If you want to turn to the left, move your hand over to your left. Then twist your hips and put pressure on the correct part of your feet (which depends on the direction you want to go). If you want to go in the direction your toes are pointed, put pressure on your toes; if you want to go in the direction your heels are pointed, put pressure on your heels. All of these movements happen in concert.

One common mistake I see is people trying to turn their boards with the upper body only. They're assuming that if they get enough momentum going with their shoulders, the board will follow. And to some degree it will, but you're not really turning the board to its optimum performance, and that will only get you so far. You'll hit a plateau; you can't progress using that technique. You've got to learn how to turn the board by weighting it, pressuring the rail, and leaning into the turn. Your feet are going to move by the nature of it, and if you ride a big board, you're going to have to move your feet a lot.

ADVANCED: THE OUTER REEFS

At the end of the day, it's all about the waves. Good waves make good surfers. If you're surfing often enough to have become proficient, your next step is to go out and find those hero waves. And make sure your passport's up-to-date, because serious surfers travel the globe looking for the best conditions. Australia, for instance, is a surfer's paradise. Indonesia: same thing. There are places in the south of France that are great. Fiji's got great surf. You go to Namotu Island, and it's like a dream. That's a surf camp and it's private, but even a relatively novice surfer will have the time of their life there.

The other thing that you need is getting out there with even better surfers. At a certain level, if you want to progress, you go to where the best guys in the world are. You watch them, and you surf with them. That will give you a good perspective of what to aspire to and how good you are—really. And then, of course, there's the "monkey see, monkey do" factor. Surf with people who know what they're doing, and it's pretty much impossible that you won't become better.

Throughout all of it, there are always the basics: your fitness level, your paddling skills, your proficiency in the ocean. How good's your car? How good's your motor? When you're strong and you have good endurance, then you can surf for 4 hours instead of 2. You can do it every day instead of every third day. The more time you can put into doing it and the harder you can do it, the faster the improvements will come.

POINTERS, SKILLS, AND THINGS TO CONSIDER

⊹ READING WAVES AND SETS When you're waiting for a wave, you have to be patient. Learn to be in the moment, and appreciate everything that's going on around you. It's an interactive relationship. After a while, reading the sets becomes instinctual.

A set can be 3 waves or 9 waves or 20 waves. It's a pulse of energy. You usually never go on the first wave (unless you know it's the biggest one) because if you fall, there will likely be a bigger one behind it. And certainly, there will be others behind it. Usually the biggest wave is the second or third one in a set, but that changes on every swell.

Reading a swell is subtle, like feeling someone's heartbeat. Storms are pulsating, and you can actually know a storm's rhythms by the swell it produces. The Polynesians were the masters of this. They had a close connection to the ocean because their survival depended on it. I think in general we've grown too far away from that. But you can develop your observational skills. You can train yourself to become excellent at seeing. The first step is to start watching as carefully as possible.

⚜ POSITION ON THE WAVE You can be on the shoulder going straight—but placing yourself 10 feet behind that position is a completely different level. That's where you're going to feel the full energy of the wave. Everyone fixates on face sizes, but I'm far more impressed by someone riding a wave that's a few feet smaller if they're riding it deeper.

⚜ CRASHING There's a real art to crashing. It's an undervalued skill. The worst place you can be is in the lip because when it breaks, it parts the water's surface. You can literally feel like you're falling onto the ground. The safest place to be is inside the wave when it's barreling because if you fall there, you can come out the back. The good news is that you won't take such a beating. The bad news is that the next one will be right there. Whatever happens when you fall, relax. It sounds counterintuitive, but fighting the ocean is pointless and just burns up your oxygen faster. If you fall in shallow water, make like a starfish to avoid hitting the bottom—spread your arms and legs to maximize your surface area. Whatever you do, don't dive off your board headfirst unless you know the water is deep enough.

GERRY LOPEZ

I've been surfing almost 50 years now. It's been pretty much my whole life, my career, all I've ever wanted to do. Surfing is a personal and private experience: just you and the ocean and your surfboard. And then the wave comes, and it's just you and the wave. You do have to pay your dues; surfing is a constant process of having the crap scared out of you. It takes a lot of work and a lot of years to get really good at it.

One thing I've experienced about surfing is that everything seems to happen faster now. Progress and development—everything is accelerated. Geez, it's really grown into quite a scene. None of us had any idea that surfing was going to be this big, but I guess it makes sense because everyone who does it understands immediately how great it is. Surfing rocks you to your core—your soul, basically.

DAVE'S
TUTORIALS

A few times each year, my friend Dave Kalama gathers a group of very lucky people together on Kauai or Maui. It's called Kalama Kamp, and among other things, it helps people become better surfers. In case you can't make it yourself, here's a sampling of Dave's wisdom so you can take notes from one of the best watermen out there.

If I were teaching you how to surf, the first thing I'd do is to make sure you can swim. Once we'd established that, I'd find a place—the south side of Maui is good—where the waves were knee- to chest-high. I like to start people off on a large board with a lot of buoyancy; that could range from 9 feet all the way up to a 12-foot board, depending on the person's size. The bigger the board, the more stable it is. And the more stable it is, the easier it is to stand up on. On the other side of that coin, the bigger the board, the harder it is to maneuver. But there's no point worrying about maneuvering if you can't stand up! Once you can get to your feet and glide along for a few yards, then you can decrease the board size a bit so you've got more control.

Before you got into the water, I'd show you how to jump to your feet, where to look, and what your body position should be. Basically, you want to look to the direction in which you want to go—similar to skiing or driving. Your focus is just beyond the nose of the board, maybe 20 feet out in front. You don't want to be looking down at your shorts or your feet or at what's behind you.

One mistake people make is that when they stand up, they get back on their heels. When you're scared and you don't know what's coming, it's a natural reaction to get into the backseat. But in that position, your balance isn't nearly as good. If the wave hits you, the board will accelerate and you'll be off the back end. So I always tell people to keep some weight on their toes. That way they're centered on their feet, with their weight balanced on both feet, and they can lean into their toes or their heels, depending on what they need to do.

Paddling skills are important. Sometimes it's a challenge just to get out to the lineup. Alternating your arms as you paddle is probably the best technique—as opposed to using both arms in tandem. It might feel rough on your chest if you're not used to lying on the board. Often, at the end of the day, a new surfer feels soreness around the rib cage. That's common. And of course your shoulders will feel it, too, if you're not used to pulling yourself through the water.

Once you've mastered paddling out, turning around, catching a wave, and riding it straight, then I would graduate you down to a 9-foot-6 board or a 10-footer. And I'd tell you to start angling to the right or the left, depending on how the wave breaks. In other words, at this point, you want to keep your board in the open face of the wave, just in front of the whitewater—that position allows you the most maneuverability to carve in the open, clean water, as opposed to when you're in the whitewater. When the water's churned up, you're pretty much stuck going straight in. So that would be the next stage, to try to ride the shoulder just in front of the whitewater.

Meanwhile, you're still centered. But now you want to start to experiment by putting more pressure on your toes and heels in order to turn the board. Essentially, when you shift more weight to one side of the board, it will turn in that direction. So if I put more weight on my toes because I'm a regular-stance surfer, that would cause the board to move to the right. And if you're a goofy-foot stance (meaning your right foot's forward), then putting weight on your toes would cause your board to turn to the left. For heels, it's the opposite.

When you're learning how to turn, you want to move back on the board in order to create thrust using the fins. Initially, you'll stand in the center, but as you start to turn, you move toward the tail a little more. As you weight one side, the nose will come up slightly, and that will cause the board to turn more sharply.

Like anything, you have to go out and experiment. In surfing there are so many things going on that it's hard to consciously dictate a sequential order of what you need to do. Your body needs to learn these movements and coordinate them on a subconscious level. There's no secret other than mileage. You've got to go out and do the hard yards and let your body figure it out. It's like learning how to walk. You've got to fall down a few times.

To become an advanced surfer, it's critical to know how to use your upper body in conjunction with your lower body. The experts use their shoulders to reinforce and accentuate what they're doing with their lower bodies and their centers of mass.

Using the whole body helps make the turn more extreme. You need to apply pressure on the rail, whether it's on your toe side or your heel side; you need to shift your weight to your front foot or back foot, depending on where you are in the turn to create drive, as opposed to just turning the nose in a different direction. And it's a really subtle thing. It requires a lot of feel. Some advanced surfers can do really tight turns, but they haven't mastered how to generate the thrust from the board to maintain that speed and go into another one. Kelly [Slater] and the guys who can generate so much speed through their turns and maintain it throughout the whole wave—that is really an art form in itself.

POINTERS, SKILLS, AND THINGS TO CONSIDER

To ride a wave, first you have to catch it. Wave selection only comes with experience. Some people catch on better than others. Essentially, it's being able to read the surface of the water. And anticipating what's going to happen based upon the shape of a wave and the direction it's traveling, and then incorporating other things like the water's texture from the wind and the bottom contours of the seafloor and how that'll affect the wave. Being able to decipher all of that just from watching the wave travel through the water takes time. The only way to learn it is by making mistakes. Once you see it coming and go for it, you'll either catch it or you'll miss it—and then, based on what happened, you adjust your plan of attack. (And of course you're not sure the next wave you see will be lined up the same way.) So in every situation you're storing the data: "Okay, it looked like this; it tapered at the ends like this; that means I should be over here." You're trying to process all this information and make a judgment so you can put yourself in the right position.

If you live in, say, Chicago, and you're not going to have the opportunity to spend a lot of time in the water—hours and hours to learn all the little idiosyncrasies of how a wave acts—then the next best thing you can do is to go to a location where the wave breaks very consistently, like at a point break. That'll give you a better chance to get more waves and more experience. (That's also why point breaks tend to be very crowded.)

Another great strategy to learn a wave is to watch the locals. There really is a home court advantage in surfing. That's why I think that Oahu is an ideal place for all levels of surfers—because there are so many people doing the same thing that you want to do. And doing it at a really high level. So that wealth of information is much more available than if you're surfing at some remote area in Mexico.

TRAINING FOR SURFING

THERE'S NOTHING BETTER FOR DEVELOPING YOUR SURFING ABILITIES THAN TO ACTUALLY GO SURFING. BUT WHEN THAT'S NOT POSSIBLE, HERE ARE A FEW THINGS YOU CAN DO TO STRENGTHEN YOUR SKILLS.

✜ **BUILD YOUR LEGS** Most experienced surfers have good arm strength because they spend so much time paddling. After all, we don't run down the court, we paddle down the court. And then when you're riding a wave, it's only for a short burst of time, maybe 10 to 30 seconds. So your legs really don't get pumped. But you do need strong legs to surf, especially in more challenging conditions. That means you have to supplement surfing with other kinds of activities. Biking's great, as is any kind of sand training, such as running on the beach or up and down the dunes. Weight lifting always works, but if you love to surf, you probably also love to be outside.

✜ **PRACTICE CROSSOVER BOARD SPORTS** Yes, you can benefit from balance training. After all, if you can do something well on one foot, you'll be able to do it amazingly well on two. But standing on one foot on a balance board while people throw tennis balls at you—while it's neurologically tricky and hard to master—won't necessarily make you a better surfer. That's a misconception people have sometimes. They don't always realize that balance training will only help your surfing if you've already got good board skills. One precedes the other. You need to know how to apply your balance properly, and you can only do that once you know how to ride.

Fortunately, there are many board sports that enable you to practice riding, and they all have benefits. At its root, surfing is a motion and a rhythm. You can do it on land as well as you can in the water.

Snowboarding, skateboarding, wakeboarding—they're all children of surfing. For me, snowboarding was an instant fit. The first time I tried it, I was in Alaska and got dropped off by helicopter in deep powder on a knife-edged peak. Luckily, it *was* just like surfing. However, if you take me to a resort where I've got to make it along a catwalk or onto a chairlift, that's harder. What felt the most natural to me was steep and deep. Likewise, someone who's a great snowboarder will learn to surf quickly. It's the exact same stance. They just have to learn paddling and wave timing, and they're set.

✥ **WORK ON YOUR WEAK SIDE** I learned to surf both directions when I grew up, so I don't really prefer one side over the other. Front side and back side both have their advantages, depending on the wave. In the same vein, good swimmers learn how to bilateral breathe, and tennis players work on both their forehand and their backhand. Being functionally ambidextrous as an athlete makes you more versatile, more balanced, more able to adapt on the fly to whatever circumstance you face. It also means you're less vulnerable to fatigue from stressing one side of your body more than the other. Make a point of practicing on your weak side until you don't have one anymore.

✥ **SWIM** Get yourself a pair of fins, and hit the water. When I learned to surf, we didn't have leashes. That made us good swimmers. Aside from making you more comfortable in the water, swimming develops the same back and arm muscles that you use for paddling.

DROPPING IN

BRETT LICKLE

Not only is Brett Lickle one of the best watermen around, he's also one of the most creative guys I know. And besides that, he's an expert on having fun. Here, he explains the Surfball Balance Training System, a tool he designed to make being on flat land (almost) as much fun as being in the waves, on the snow, or in the half-pipe.

✠ The Surfball System combines balance, agility, strength, toning, and surfing exercises. It's designed to give people muscle memory relative to action sports. If you think about it, a typical surf session doesn't give you that much time on your board. With the Surfball, you can get as many "waves" as you want and fine-tune your skills.

✠ It's very sport specific to what I call side stance riding. That's surfing, wakeboarding, waterskiing, snowboarding, kiting, skate-boarding, and windsurfing.

✠ A lot of times you can't practice the sport you have a passion for. And that's really what the Surfball is all about. You have 360 degrees of axis, meaning that when you stand on the ball, you have toe pressures, heel pressures, and front and back foot pressures—the same way you do on a wave or on the snow. It gives you the ability to work the muscles that are relevant to your sport.

‡ Surfball gives you a far better core workout than something like doing crunches. It puts every muscle and ligament to work while you're balancing—not to mention that it's a lot more fun.

‡ You can do a squat on it, and when you do, your legs are working 360 degrees because you're not on a stable platform. So it is a far more dynamic squat. You can get into the basic grabs on the board, where you come down and touch the board in different areas, which works different parts of your body.

In all sports, it's an asset to be ambidextrous, and this is something you can practice on the Surfball. If you're a regular-foot surfer, then learn how to train your goofy foot because that'll work the other side of your body and another part of your brain.

1. **THE BOARD** A unique depression in the bottom of the board helps control the ball while the surfer maintains balance. The depression and the ball work synergistically; each change in stance creates different balance effects. The boards are hand shaped and glassed using molded fiberglass sandwich construction; the standard board is 4 feet 10 inches long and 17 inches wide, but different lengths and shapes are available.

2. **THE ADJUSTABLE BALL** You can adjust the diameter and pressure of the ball to change the skill level required to balance. Low pressure is easiest, and you can work up from there.

3. **THE STABILITY BOWL** The bowl is designed to help first-time riders master the basics of three-dimensional balance. As you progress, you can also use the system without the bowl.

4. **THE PUMP** This adjusts ball pressure and degree of challenge.

THE STANDUP
EVOLUTION

I CALL STANDUP SURFING THE ANCIENT SPORT THAT WE'VE NEVER SEEN BUT THAT WE KNOW EXISTED. IT'S PRIMITIVE, CLASSIC, AND AT THE SAME TIME ULTRAMODERN. AND IT'S CHANGED MY LIFE IN A DOZEN DIFFERENT WAYS.

Standup paddling represents nothing less than a renewal of my excitement for surfing. After 42 years of riding, it's brought me back to a place where I can be happy on a 1-foot wave. Like yoga or tai chi, standup is one of those pursuits that looks simple—until you try it. Most people can get up and paddle around almost instantly, but once you start refining it, you can keep improving forever. After 7 years of standup, I'm still hungry to get out there because there are so many nuances to learn.

And then, of course, there's the fitness element. Standup is such an all-encompassing workout that it represents the best training for big wave riding I've ever come across. In a normal surfing situation, if you catch a long ride, that's 20 seconds. When you're standup surfing, you're out there for 2 or 3 hours (or longer), standing, working your legs, core, and foundation the entire time. And that's before you add the challenge of maneuvering a giant board. Turning a 12-foot standup board takes tremendous foot strength, balance, and coordination, and the paddle work engages your upper body and abs as well.

There's a real Zen aspect to standup. You start thinking about anything other than balancing on that board, you'll flip yourself into the water. Also, if you want it to be, this is a very calming sport. Since you can do it in any conditions and on any body of water, standup brings you into a variety of places and situations that you wouldn't otherwise get to experience. I find myself in all kinds of different parts of the ocean now, and when you spend most of your life out there, it's encouraging to have a new way to do it.

The position of standing up is a position of confidence. That's when our species evolved, when we stood up on our hind legs and started to walk and run. To be on the water that way makes you feel superconfident. You feel secure, you're not in the water, and you're not worried about what might be lurking around under there.

Since I started standup paddling, I've been able to look into the ocean like I never have before. When you're standing 6 feet off the surface, your visibility increases dramatically. You see everything—dolphins, fish, stingrays, all the sea creatures. Half of the standup experience is what you see and how that makes you feel. I told somebody recently that if I just paddled out and paddled in—never caught a wave—it would be a great day. And usually in surfing, that wouldn't be a great day. That would be a pretty discouraging day. Standup makes those dreary days bright.

To my mind, with all of this sport's dimension, the future of standup surfing is unlimited. I've ridden tidal bores in Alaska, paddled down the Colorado through the Grand Canyon, traversed the Hawaiian Island chain, crossed the English Channel, tooled around in the Mentawais; I've seen some of the most stunning scenery and visions I'll never forget while getting in my best shape and riding some of the most exhilarating waves of my life—what more could you ask for?

DAVE *KALAMA* ON STANDUP PADDLING/SURFING

One of the most appealing things about standup is how many more dimensions there are to it than to regular shortboarding. First of all, the boards are bigger and don't fit into a wave's angles quite as easily. On a shortboard, you can adjust to conditions on the fly— you might need a second or two. On a standup board, you need more like 5 or 6 seconds. So you've got to anticipate what the wave's going to do that much farther down the line. And of course with standup surfing, you're using a paddle. Essentially, you've got another arm, one that's three times longer than your normal arm. That gives you huge maneuvering ability, but handling the paddle is a skill in its own right. You can use it to catch yourself from falling over; you can use it to recover from an off the lip or a cutback or to get through flat sections. The paddle alone adds so many facets.

You also have to consider the larger planing area on a standup board: How do you get a 4-inch rail down into the water to carve a turn versus a shortboard's ¾-inch rail? The dynamics are extremely different. All of these things take time and experience to learn, and then you have to combine them all into one sequence, like a dance. It seems like such a simple movement, but the entire body is involved, transferring the energy of the paddle through your palms, your forearms, your shoulders, and your core and into your legs, to transfer that pulling motion into the board so it moves forward. If you don't orchestrate everything properly, you'll only get half the energy out of your paddle stroke.

STANDUP PADDLING

✤ I think of traditional surfing and standup surfing as akin to skiing and snowboarding. They're two different disciplines, and you don't need to know one in order
to appreciate or learn the other. Knowing how to surf is certainly not a prerequisite
for standup paddling.

✤ The beauty of standup is that it can be learned in a controlled situation. That's why
it's so appropriate for any ability level, any age—anyone who wants to get out on the
water and do something on his own terms in a very safe way. You can go down to
the back bay where the water's like a mirror and enjoy it just as much as someone
who's in the surf. Everyone finds their own level, but their sense of enjoyment is the
same. And it's the single best exercise that I've ever done. The balance involves your
entire body as well as your subconscious mind.

✤ Starting out, I always recommend you use the absolute biggest foam surfboard you
can find. That'll make it easier to learn the balance dynamics. The introduction
usually takes people a few moments because they're not used to standing on something so tippy. But when you get used to it and your body reacts more quickly, all of

a sudden it begins to feel stable or relatively stable. So start out with something big; somewhere around 29 to 34 inches wide and 12 to 13 feet long. The larger and heavier you are, the wider and longer you want the board to be. Once you get going, you can reevaluate your board size and shape. If paddling around is all that you're looking for, there's no need to change to a skinnier or smaller board. If your goal is to get into the surf, then you'll want to graduate down to boards that are smaller so you can maneuver better. If your goal is to paddle from one island to the next, you'll want to work your way into the longer boards, say, 14- to 18-foot lengths. They're

DROPPING IN

DAVE KALAMA

Many surfers feel that how they ride a wave is how everyone should ride a wave. But there are so many different ways to surf, and they're all fun: bodysurfing, windsurfing, canoe surfing, foilboarding, standup surfing, tow surfing, kite surfing. If you keep an open mind, you end up spending so much more time in the water. And what's really great is that trying something one way can teach you how to make all the other ways better—and then you can even start inventing your own techniques, adapting your equipment. A true waterman is always learning, always changing, always experimenting.

much sleeker through the water. So you can see that there are many different options. And they're all a blast.

‡ Stand with your feet parallel to each other and shoulder-width apart. You want your big toes to land right at the center of the board. Measure either from the tip or the tail, and then make a little mark as a reference point. Put your big toes at that line. When you get more experienced, you might move a few inches forward or back, depending on where the flotation sits in the board, but as a rule of thumb, that's a real safe place to start.

‡ The standup paddle stroke is similar to a canoe paddle stroke. Reach out as far in front of you as you can, dig the paddle down into the water—submerge the blade completely—and pull back. There's no need to stroke farther than your feet because once the angle of the paddle goes past vertical, you're actually slowing yourself down. At your feet, slide the paddle out to the side in a smooth recovery. It doesn't need to come out high; it just needs to barely stay above the surface of the water.

‡ When you're paddling downwind and you're actually riding little swells, then you'll want to move back on the board a few inches. When it's planing, you need to keep the nose up so you don't pearl. And if you catch a wave, you'll definitely want to scoot back quite a bit.

‡ Because you're standing upright as you paddle out, you have a much better view of what's coming in from the ocean. You can see the waves long before the guys who are sitting down on their boards can see them. And the paddle, once you learn how to use it, gives you far more thrust to catch the wave. But having both of those things to your advantage can also work against you if you catch too many waves in a popular surf spot. In other words, be respectful of the surfers who are out there with you. Standup boards are bigger, they're harder to control, and they're much heavier, so they're dangerous to people around you (and yourself). I generally tell people to stay away from popular surfing spots on a standup board. Go out where there's nobody else around. You can fall and you're not going to endanger anybody.

BOARD *GAMES*

At the risk of sounding biased—which I am—and also of being sued by Nike for copyright infringement, when it comes to standup, these three words come to mind: Just do it. All you need is a board and a paddle. Here are a few notes to keep in mind when you're thinking about equipment.

STANDUP BOARDS AND PADDLES

You want to find the calmest water, initially, to learn. Don't start in the surf. You'll need a board with enough flotation and stability for your size and a paddle that's approximately 8 to 10 inches taller than your height. A 12-foot board works for almost everyone. You've got to weigh more than 300 pounds to need something larger.

My **paddle** is about a foot taller than I am because I lift my hand high when I paddle. When you're learning, you don't want to lift your hand that high because it raises your center of gravity. And it puts a lot of stress on your shoulder.

The **paddle blade** has a 7- to 10-degree angle. This enables the blade to stay square to the water for a longer period of time. People have an instinctive tendency to hold the paddle backward because they're trying to "hook" the water. But it's held the other way around.

Quick Blade makes my paddles. There are various shapes available, and I've gravitated toward certain ones that I like. There's a beginner shape, an intermediate shape, and then one for big waves.

A **standup board**'s different than a regular surfboard. It has a different shape, different rocker. You can't stand on a regular surfboard because it doesn't have enough flotation.

My production boards, which are made by Surftech, range in size from 10 to 12 feet.

The stance is different than surfing in that you're squared off. You stand exactly like a downhill skier. Two feet, side by side, pointing forward in the middle of the board. You hold the paddle with one hand at the top and one in the middle. In the beginning, you'll be switching hands a lot because you won't know how to make the board go straight yet. After a while you'll learn how to maneuver the board without having to switch sides all the time. It has to do with your balance on the board. Normally you weight the side you're paddling on, but that's a bit tricky when you're just learning.

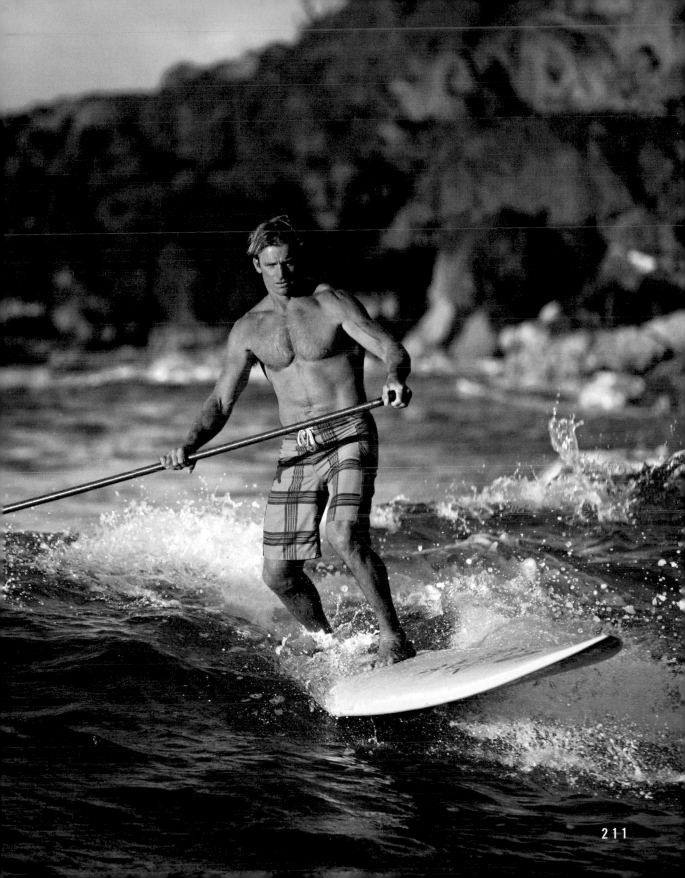

FOILBOARDING

Contrary to what you may have heard, there are no bad waves. In all conditions, there's a perfect way to ride every wave—you just have to adapt. Hydrofoil surfing, or foilboarding (or foiling, for short), was created with that goal in mind; like tow surfing, it's a tool that enables us to take advantage of conditions that would otherwise go unridden. The foilboard is a surfboard that's modified with a rudder, and the two are connected by a vertical strut.

With foiling, none of the usual rules apply. You can ride waves that don't break—that alone allows you a whole new way of looking at the ocean: learning to read the subtleties of how a swell rolls and moves rather than reacting to something more obvious, like a breaking wave. You can ride at places that aren't even surf spots, and you can ride a wave for 10 miles if you want to. And because the board floats above the water's surface, the surfer rides above the chop, above the friction. You can be on the roughest storm wave ever and it feels like you're on a magic carpet.

Most people, when they first see the foilboard, can't figure out how it works. The best way to describe it is that the foil acts like a miniature underwater glider. As the surfer moves in one direction, the wave's energy presses from the opposite direction, generating lift (exactly as a thermal air current would) so the surfboard rises off the surface.

It's the single most efficient wave-riding instrument we've been able to experience to date, but right now we're in kindergarten. We are not doing calculus yet. I know it will evolve. We're constantly tinkering with the boards, but it takes time to develop equipment properly. Today we have a board that works well, but it could go further. If you think about bicycles, what we've got is a unicycle.

The most important thing about the foilboard is that it's a fresh way of looking at riding. All the different disciplines—from bodysurfing to standup to foiling—enhance one another. Each one makes you better at the next. And if you put them all together, not only will you become a better all-around surfer, but when everyone else is sitting around on shore complaining about the "crappy" conditions, you won't have to listen. You'll be in the water.

MY *FAVORITE* BOARDS

Making a great surfboard is an art, and there's a mystique to it. If I take my favorite board, send it to a computerized shaping machine, and have it mastered down to the millimeter—doesn't work. It's not the same. I might try 10 boards and not like any of them. And then I'll get one that's just magic.

1. CROSSING STANDUP PADDLE BOARD

Length: 16 feet

Weight: 28 pounds

Used for: paddling 500 miles across the Hawaiian Islands

In May 2006, I made a 270-mile, 2-day London-to-Paris crossing, paddling the English Channel after riding a bike from London to Dover, and then from the French coast to the Arc de Triomphe. That was a longtime goal, and I used the journey as a chance to raise awareness and money for autism. In October, Dave Kalama and I decided to create an even bigger challenge for ourselves: to paddle from the Big Island of Hawaii to Maui, Lanai, Molokai, Oahu, and finally Kauai, riding bikes over the land portion of the trip. Between these two crossings, we raised over $100,000 for the cause (see page 167).

One thing that's unusual about this board is its foot rudders. Their purpose is to counteract the prevailing winds, which in Hawaii generally come from the northeast. In the open ocean, you need to be able to paddle on both sides of your body, so it's important to be able to steer with the feet—especially if the board is this long. I designed it using solo canoes and ocean kayaks as a reference. It has its own custom travel case, but, needless to say, flying around with a 16-foot board isn't easy.

2. PE'AHI STANDUP GUN

Length: 13 feet

Weight: 38 pounds

Used for: standup surfing at Pe'ahi, the wave on Maui that's also known as Jaws.

I have two identical boards like this, shaped by Ron House. They're unique because they're 13-foot guns—an enlarged version of what we lay on at Waimea years ago, before we started towing. So they're retro in that sense, but they're also very forward because they're used for standup paddling. These boards are tippy because of their outline, but the weight gives them some stability.

3. STANDUP PADDLE BOARD

Length: 12 feet

Weight: 28 pounds

Used for: paddling across the English Channel

This is Surftech's production standup board. It's wide and stable—really an oversize traditional longboard. I think of this as the board that made standup paddling possible. It was modeled from one of the original prototypes that I worked with shapers to design. Throughout the evolution of standup paddling, Bill Hamilton, Gerry Lopez, Ron House, Dick Pearson, and Dick Brewer all created boards. They're the most talented shapers in the world. I've worked with all of them throughout my life.

I used this particular board to paddle across the English Channel (see page 45), which took 7 hours. A lot of standup boards have decking on them, so you don't need to use wax, but I grew up with wax, and I like the feel of it. This is a great board for anyone who wants to get into standup. You have to weigh more than 300 pounds for it not to work for you.

4. TEAHUPOO TOW BOARD

Length: 6 feet 10 inches

Weight: 16 pounds

Used for: riding waves too massive to paddle into

This board was made by my dad, Bill Hamilton. Over the years he's made many of my boards. He's a master. I used this board when I first surfed big Teahupoo in 2000. People always ask what it's like to surf a wave that intense, but it's impossible to describe in words. It'd be like trying to describe, say, the color purple. The moment demands so much focus that you can't think of anything else. Time stops. Before I rode this board in Tahiti, I rode it at Jaws. It has a three-fin configuration, and the fins are glassed on, which seems prehistoric now. These days our fins are made of metal so they can be thinner and shorter with no loss of performance. They're virtually cavitation free at any speed now.

5. CURRENT TOW BOARD

Length: 6 feet 2 inches

Weight: approximately 25 pounds

Used for: Time will tell!

There are endless variables in making a great tow board. It's a complex combination of construction, wood, blank, and glassing, combined with outline, thickness, flow, rocker, weight-to-volume ratio, and fin configuration. My tow boards are relatively light because of my body mass. You need a solid amount of weight to make it down the face of an 80-foot wave, but at the same time, you want the least possible amount of surface area to minimize friction. If the board's too light, you'll be sucked back up the face. This board was shaped by Dick Brewer, who's like the genius of all shapers. He's taught everybody. He taught my dad; he taught Gerry Lopez.

The foot straps were a key part of our evolution. They give you leverage. Normally, when you stand on a board, you can press with your heels and press with your toes. When you add foot straps, you can press with your heels and *lift* with your toes. That gives you double the amount of edge pressure. Some surfers don't use heel straps, but I do. I like them because they give you more intimacy with the board. And they give you something extra to push against. But the downside is if you fall, it's harder to get out.

6. HYDROFOIL BOARD [CENTER]

Length: 4 feet

Weight: 42 pounds—which is nothing

Used for: extrarough conditions, long rolling swells (see page 213)

The foilboard is a hybrid, invented by tinkering around in the garage. Hybrids are nice because you're taking existing technology and products and combining them to create a new way of doing something. To ride this board, we use snowboard boots. Obviously we don't need them to be as bulky as they are because we're not in cold environments. But companies have spent millions of dollars designing these boots. They're buoyant, and they have a quick-release system. Best of all, they already exist. You're not waiting for a prototype to come, and then you break it the next day and it takes 4 months to get another one. It's like, why reinvent the wheel?

With this board you can go to places that aren't even surf spots—and as the water gets more crowded, that's appealing. If you wanted to, you could ride a wave for 10 miles. Foiling is like flying without the consequences of crashing.

DROPPING IN

ROB MACHADO

Now that I'm not surfing competitively anymore [after 15 years on the pro tour], it's really freed my mind to search out the art side of surfing. All the different things that people are doing on surfboards—it's as though they're different artists. That's surfing to me; it's riding anything and everything that's out there. It all comes back to being in the ocean, being in the water— the pure joy I get out of feeling that energy. People ask me if I'm retired, but what they don't realize is that I'm going to be surfing my entire life. Whether I'm boogie boarding a wave when I'm 90 years old, bodysurfing, whatever it is, I'll be in the ocean enjoying it somewhere, somehow.

ON *TOW* SURFING

KNOW BEFORE *YOU* *TOW*

The Nietzsche quote says it all about how the intelligent rider approaches tow surfing: one step at a time, slowly. It's definitely not something to rush into, and unfortunately, these days many surfers are doing that. To put this discipline into perspective, here's a brief history of the sport, along with Dave Kalama's and my observations and advice about why, when, where, and how someone should (or should not) bring out the Jet Ski.

LAIRD: My father, Bill Hamilton, was a competitive surfer in the '60s. I watched him compete in contests and decided at a young age that I didn't want anything to do with those kinds of events. Competition brought out the aggressive side of me, and I'm aggressive enough already. I wanted to make surfing more of an artistic expression.

Eventually, I started windsurfing. With the sails, we could put ourselves into really good position far offshore. That was exciting, and a light went off in our heads: If we could drag ourselves onto little waves, we could probably drag ourselves onto some really big ones. But the problem with using a windsurfer to do that was the sail. It could help you catch the wave, but then you had to deal with this awkward thing on the way down. Eventually we used a Zodiac and then a Jet Ski to get towed onto waves. That was the best of both worlds—it eliminated the sail and still gave us the power we needed.

And thus was born tow surfing: the art of using a mechanically powered craft to propel yourself onto waves in conditions that are physically unrealistic, impossible to catch manually. Waves that would otherwise go unridden by the best surfers in the world.

About eight of us got together and developed the equipment and the safety protocols.

There were Darrick Doerner, Brett Lickle, Sierra Emory, Mike Waltse, Buzzy Kerbox, Dave Kalama, Mark Angulo, Rush Randle, and me. We weren't out to impress anybody. I loved the shoulder. We were there in a relatively safe place, climbing the ladder rung by rung, getting more comfortable. And so now, when someone says, "Oh, my gosh, look how high you are!" I don't feel so high because I've taken it one step at a time. It's not like you just jump up to the top of the ladder. It's a progression. After boot camp, you don't immediately become a general.

DAVE: The first requirement for tow surfing is that you need to be a really solid swimmer. You should be comfortable with swimming out into 15- to 20-foot surf (in Hawaii that means 30- to 40-foot faces) and know that you can swim back in through the lineup. And even though no one is truly relaxed swimming in through 40-foot faces, you should be confident that "yes, I'll survive this. I can make it. I'll probably take a pounding, but it's something I can do." Because at some point you will be in that situation. Even as maneuverable as the Jet Skis are and as expertly as people can drive, it's going to happen. You do everything you can to minimize the chances that it will happen—but it will happen. So you've got to be prepared for that in terms of survival.

LAIRD: Unless you can ride 30-foot surf paddling in on your stomach, you shouldn't be on a line. If you're not capable of riding a 30-foot face manually, there's no way in the world you should be out there towing behind a Jet Ski.

Really good surfers are the slowest guys to tow because they have the most respect for the surf. Guys that don't have the experience—their naïveté is their shelter. They go in there and don't know any better. They don't realize how heavy the wave is until they get pounded and broken and bust up, and then they might not recover, either psychologically or physically. Towing's a whole other beast.

DAVE: You have to learn to see. Guys who really know what they're doing are aware of everything that's going on around them. Usually, there are only a few people out there who have that sense, who know how much time they have to go in and get someone if they need to, know that there are 10 boats in the channel and on how many of the boats the captains are capable of doing anything if you needed help, know who will become a risk if he moves over this way—and just have a good time-space relationship with the wave and everybody around it. It's hard for me to say that's something you can learn. Either you have it or you don't.

Laird and I and the rest of the gang—we'd go out every day if it was big enough. We didn't just wait for the nice days or when the cameramen could be there. Every single day we went; we made the mistakes that you have to make in order to get up the mountain. It's a little trite, but I always say: It's only a mistake if you don't learn from it. Every mishap is just a lesson we need to learn to avoid learning it farther down the line in a situation that could be really harmful. Just putting those miles in day after day.

What's happening now is that on big days, guys are trying to learn their ABCs when they should already be at XYZ. Unfortunately, all the pictures and the videos make it look easy—and it's not. They see the pictures of a giant wave and it's sunny, you're carving a nice turn, the colors are beautiful, and it's the centerfold of the magazine, and they think, *Okay, all I've got to do is drop in, make it to the bottom, turn to the right, and I'm up! Put me in the magazine.* They don't see all the hard yards and the practice and the wrecked skis on the rocks that it took to get to that point.

LAIRD: Probably the most important thing to ask yourself is why you want to tow surf. In a heavy situation, the most critical part of someone's reaction is why they're out there in the first place. If their intentions are pure, they'll react well when the shit hits the fan. They'll be cool, calm, and do the right thing. But if they're out there for selfish ambitions and other ulterior motives—anything other than that they love it and want to experience this unique thing in the ocean—then they're going to endanger everybody.

DAVE: A tow surfer becomes a really good tow surfer by doing his homework. Finding a partner you can trust is important. And one that has the same aspirations that you do. That way you can climb the mountain together. Because you don't want a partner who says, "You know what? If I make it to base camp, that's as far as I need to go. I'll be the happiest camper in the world." And you're thinking, *Well, I want to get up to the peak!* As soon as you get past the base camp, there's going to be a little dysfunction going on! Pick a partner who has the same goals so you can work together all the way.

PE'AHI: MY GIRL

WITH APOLOGIES TO MY WIFE AND DAUGHTERS (BUT I KNOW THEY UNDERSTAND).

Pe'ahi is the name of a wave that breaks about a mile from my house in Maui. It's also known as Jaws, but that's just the media's name for it. No matter what you call it, this is a rare spot. It has always been considered sacred, in the past by the ancient Hawaiians; in the present, by us. Most of the time if you looked out at Pe'ahi, you wouldn't even know it was there. Only the largest swells cause it to break, and so we get to ride it only a handful of times every year. When Pe'ahi goes off, its faces can be 70 to 80 feet high.

The ability to surf this location at all resulted from our desire to catch waves that were considered unrideable because of their size and speed. Through that desire we developed tow surfing, the technique of using a Jet Ski to actually pull us into these waves. In 1994 that led us to Pe'ahi, which in Hawaiian means "the beacon" or "the calling." When you live near it and you surf it, you know that its name is true: On the nights before a big day, you can hear it rumbling in the distance. And it calls you.

This wave definitely speaks to my soul. I'm drawn to it because I know that any experience I have out there is going to be one I'll remember. Surfing it brings feelings of accomplishment, of fear, and of reverence for its beauty and power—but even looking at it blows me away. Brett Lickle, who's been riding this wave with me since the beginning, refers to it as the Great Mother. I agree. She's right in my backyard, and yet in a million years I could never take her for granted.

The Strapped Crew

www.lairdhamilton.com
www.watermanfilm.com
www.gotogabby.com

BODY

Training

Paul Chek, CHEK Institute
www.chekinstitute.com
800-552-8789

T. R. Goodman
Pro Camp Sports
www.procampsports.com
310-664-9908

Nadia Toraman
www.maui-yoga.com
808-283-4123

Eating

Giada De Laurentiis
www.giadadelaurentiis.com

Bui Sushi
310-456-1500

Neuro 1
www.nutrition53.com

Catie's Organic Greens; Catie's Organic
Vitamin C Plus
www.energyessentials.com
818-591-9355

Udo's Oils
www.udoschoice.com

Muscle Milk
www.cytosport.com

For exotic and unique sea salts:
www.saltistry.com

For guidelines on sustainable
harvested fish:
www.montereybayaquarium.org

Anthony's Coffee Co.
www.anthonyscoffee.com
800-882-6509

Recovering

Game Ready
www.gameready.com

Dr. Neal S. ElAttrache, Kerlan-Jobe
Orthopaedic Clinic, Los Angeles
www.kerlan-jobe.com

SOUL

For environmental groups dealing with ocean issues:
www.nrdc.org/oceans
www.oceana.org
www.surfaidinternational.org
www.surfrider.org

For more information about the Japanese dolphin slaughter:
www.savejapandolphins.org

For more information about plastic pollution in the ocean:
www.algalita.org

For more information about mercury pollution in the ocean:
www.oceana.org

Beautiful Son
www.beautifulson.com

Talk About Curing Autism (TACA)
www.talkaboutcuringautism.org

National Autism Foundation
www.nationalautismassociation.org

SURFING

For more information about Dave Kalama and Kalama Kamps:
www.davekalama.com
808-760-2224

For more information about Brett Lickle and the Surfball Balance Training System:
www.surfball.net

Gerry Lopez
www.gerrylopezsurfboards.com

Rob Machado
www.robmachado.com

Surftech
www.surftech.com
831-479-4944

QuickBlade
www.quickbladepaddles.com
888-295-0482

Oxbow
www.oxboworld.com

Wonderwall
www.thisiswonderwall.com

Becker Surfboards
www.beckersurf.com
888-673-0225

Surfline
www.surfline.com
714-374-0556

H2O Audio
www.h2oaudio.com

PHOTO CREDITS

Pages ii–iii: © Tony Friedkin/Sony Pictures Classics/ZUMA/Corbis

Page viii: © Nino Munoz

Pages x, 39, 41, 42, 43, 45, 46, 65, 89: © Kurt Markus

Pages xii, 16, 18, 19, 23, 70–75, 79–87, 94–95, 166, 170, 178–179, 190, 193, 199, 211, 212, 214: © Don King

Pages xiv–1, 14, 34–35, 162, 165, 189, 200, 208–209, 218: © Tom Servais

Pages 2, 140–141, 173, 187, 195, 196, 206, 224, 226–227, 231, 232–233, 234: © Erik Aeder

Pages 4, 5, 180–181: © Darrell Wong

Pages 6, 9, 68–69, 177, 182, 188: © Tim McKenna

Pages 10, 24–25, 67, 91, 144, 174: © David Turnley/Contour by Getty Images

Pages 12, 15, 121: © Sam Jones/Corbis Outline

Pages 21, 219, 220: © Sylvain Cazenave

Page 30: © Sylvain Cazenave/Corbis Outline

Pages 32–33, 153: Courtesy of Susan Casey

Page 36: © Peggy Sirota/Corbis Outline

Pages 48, 202: © Jeff Hornbaker

Pages 52 59, 103, 104: © Joan Allen

Pages 60, 63: Courtesy of T.R. Goodman

Page 76: © Coe Huston

Pages 92, 142–143, 147: © John Russell

Page 98: Courtesy of Dr. Neal ElAttrache

Page 101: © Anthony Mandler/Corbis Outline

Page 111: © Lisa Romerein/The Image Bank/Getty Images

Page 118: Courtesy of the C.H.E.K. Institute

Page 122: Courtesy of Ed and Keri Stewart

Page 125: © FoodPhotography Eising/StockFood Creative/Getty Images

Page 128: © www.splashnews.com

Page 129: Courtesy of Giada De Laurentiis

Pages 131, 133, 135, 137, 139: Photography © Mitch Mandel/Rodale Images, Food Styling by Diane Vezza

Page 148: © Rick Doyle/Corbis

Pages 154, 157, 161, 228: Courtesy of Laird Hamilton

Page 158: © Jeff Hornbaker/Contour by Getty Images

INDEX

Boldface page references indicate photographs. <u>Underscored</u> references indicate boxed text.